THE HUMAN BEING FULLY ALIVE

Writings in celebration
of Brian Thorne

EDITOR
JEFF LEONARDI

PCCS BOOKS
Ross-on-Wye

First published 2010

PCCS BOOKS Ltd.
2 Cropper Row
Alton Road
Ross-on-Wye
Herefordshire
HR9 5LA
UK
Tel +44 (0)1989 763 900
www.pccs-books.co.uk

The Human Being Fully Alive: Writings in Celebration of Brian Thorne

A CIP catalogue record for this book is available from the British Library

ISBN 978 1 906254 34 6

Cover image *Matisse Dancers* © Janyt Piercy, mixed media artist www.artspace05.com
Cover designed in the UK by Old Dog Graphics
Printed by Imprint.Digital.net, Exeter, UK

CONTENTS

This book is dedicated to Jean Clark:
therapist, poet and writer

Introduction

Jeff Leonardi

The glory of God is a human being fully alive. (Irenaeus)

Brian Thorne, Emeritus Professor of Counselling at the University of East Anglia, Professor of Education in the College of Teachers, Co-founder of the Norwich Centre for Personal and Professional Development and Lay Canon of Norwich Cathedral, is one of the brightest stars in the firmament of the school of counselling and psychotherapy known as the Person-centred approach, founded by Professor Carl Rogers. Over his professional life he has been a teacher, counsellor, group facilitator, trainer, supervisor, director of a counselling agency, lecturer and spiritual companion, and continues to be many if not most of these, even after retiring from full-time work. His recent focus has been towards the latter end of this spectrum, that of spiritual accompanying, and he has recently developed, with others, the Diploma in Spiritual Accompaniment at the Norwich Centre for Personal and Professional Development, which offers so much of its existence and development to him.

Brian has had an immense impact in the whole field of counselling studies internationally and in Britain and has had enormous significance for at least two generations of students and staff at UEA and further afield. He has been a pioneer in introducing and developing the Person-centred approach, and was a well respected colleague of Carl Rogers himself in many international workshops until the latter's death in 1987. He has also written a significant biography of Rogers (Thorne 1992). In many ways, Brian's most distinctive contributions to the development of the Person-centred approach have been in the ways he has recognised, affirmed and developed the spiritual dimension of the Person-centred approach. Spirituality is an area of human life and awareness which has inestimable importance for huge numbers of human beings. Defined most broadly as *that which gives value, meaning and purpose to human existence*, it is hard to conceive of any human being who would not acknowledge its significance; but even understood more precisely in terms of a sense of coherence and purpose in all things, a sense of transcendence and the numinous – but as yet with no invocation of the 'God' word – a very high proportion of the world's population will affirm such a dimension of their experience of reality, and this before 'religion' or 'faith' has been introduced into the discussion.

It is clear that counselling and psychotherapy, as disciplines which seek to engage with the deepest levels of human consciousness and relationship, must deliberately and positively seek to cater for these dimensions of humanness. Brian Thorne's contribution to this process has not been simply to cater for such spiritual awareness, but to reveal the extent to which they are so often present in the counselling process and relationship. In 1982 he wrote about the concept of *Intimacy* (Thorne 1982), and in 1985 this was further developed as *The Quality of Tenderness* (Thorne 1985). Students of the Person-centred approach will know that any suggestion that the *Core Conditions* of a helping relationship (empathy, genuineness and acceptance, for short) were not simply necessary and sufficient, but might need augmenting with a further condition, was provocative to say the least! Actually Thorne's description of this quality of tenderness was utterly consistent with Rogers' own testimony. Where Rogers refers to what can occur at points of deep inner- and other-connectedness:

> When I am at my best, as a group facilitator or as a therapist … when I am closest to my inner, intuitive self, when I am somehow in touch with the unknown in me, when perhaps I am in a slightly altered state of consciousness, then, whatever I do seems to be full of healing. Then, simply my presence is releasing and helpful to the other … it seems that my inner spirit has reached out and touched the inner spirit of the other. Our relationship transcends itself and becomes a part of something larger. Profound growth and healing and energy are present. (Rogers, 1980, p. 129)

Thorne develops this into an examination of what this 'quality of presence' might signify, and suggests a name for it: not just *presence* but *tenderness*. When tenderness was present, perhaps as an outcome of the core conditions, 'something qualitatively different may occur':

> It seems as if for a space, however brief, two human beings are fully alive, because they have given themselves and each other permission to risk being fully alive. At such a moment, I have no hesitation in saying that my client and I are caught up in a stream of love. Within this stream, there comes an effortless or intuitive understanding and what is astonishing is how complex this understanding can be. It sometimes seems that I receive my client whole and thereafter possess a knowledge of him or her which does not depend on biographical data. This understanding is intensely personal and invariably it affects the self-perception of the client and can lead to marked changes in attitude and behaviour. For me as a counsellor, it is accompanied by a sense of joy which, when I have checked it out, has always been shared by the client. (Thorne, 1991, p. 77)

Thorne develops his understanding of the spirituality of such experiences in terms of their representing an antidote to the legacy of shame and guilt from which so many suffer and which is so potently expressed in the biblical narrative of the Fall: the loss of trust in God and therefore in ourselves as his creatures; in our bodies, sexuality and desires, our very freedom of will. Thorne's claim is that in these moments of freedom and intimacy this legacy is overcome:

> For a moment, shame gives way to wholeness and the liberating paradox, and at this moment God is trustworthy, the body is trustworthy, desires are trustworthy, sexuality is not a problem, survival is not a problem, death is not to be dreaded. For a moment, perhaps a fraction of a second, we are transformed and utterly free of shame. We are restored to full friendship with God or, in secular terms, we know that we are born to be lovers and to be loved. That which I have described as qualitatively different has happened and we are never quite the same again, however much we forget, deny or deride the experience. (Thorne, ibid, p. 80)[1]

---

1. These aspects of Thorne's work are further developed in Chapter 3.

It will now be evident to the reader who is not familiar with Thorne's work that we are dealing with a therapist and writer of considerable depth, not just of psychology, but also of spirituality, and indeed theology. The references to the Fall narrative and the way in which human beings can be prone to a reduced version of their humanity by its application, consciously or culturally, and the ways in which transformative relationship can overcome and heal this legacy, are a happy challenge to all systems of belief and their application.

Personal connections

I have known Brian Thorne for over thirty years. I first met him at a Person-centred 'Cross Cultural Communications Workshop', led by Carl Rogers and an international team of facilitators including Brian, in Spain in 1979, during my initial counsellor training. He impressed me then as exemplifying an attitude of unconditional acceptance and compassion which was undergirded by an evident spirituality. Our relationship developed in a variety of Person-centred contexts over subsequent years, but then when I began to contemplate undertaking doctoral research in the field of Person-centred and Christian spirituality, Brian emerged as the obvious candidate for Supervisor, and eventually we embarked on what turned out to be a nine-year journey of part-time study for me, and of faithful and painstaking supervision for him.

I was awarded my doctorate in 2009 (Leonardi 2008). My gratitude to Brian for his part in that achievement is enormous, and the presentation of this collection is in part a way of expressing my thanks and appreciation to him. Even more importantly I believe that it constitutes a body of work which affirms the fundamental value and significance of that 'intangible' spirituality, whose ignoring or denial can so damage and impoverish the human condition. The writers represented here all declare their allegiance to this theme in their own way and affirm the importance for them of Brian Thorne's personhood, life and work.

It was never the intention with this collection that it should amount to a series of personal tributes to Brian, the person and professional, as such, although there are many references to his importance to individual contributors. Rather the intention was to invite each contributor to submit a piece from their own perspective, whose substance reflected their own development in relation to the themes that Brian Thorne has so powerfully and faithfully developed in his body of work. In that sense, each contribution honours Brian's work even more by affirming the integrity of those themes in the life, work and experience of each contributor.

The title of this collection, *The Human Being Fully Alive,* is taken from a quotation of St Irenaeus: 'The glory of God is a human being fully alive'. If I owe an especial debt to Brian Thorne in my understanding of spirituality, it is most closely encapsulated in the recognition of what it means to be 'truly human'. The Lichfield Diocesan programme of local ministry training includes a module on various theories of faith development. Before the students look at the theories of faith development proposed by e.g., Fowler and Westerhoff, they are encouraged to explore their own life- and faith-journeys.

One of the early exercises in the module invites participants to depict their images of God at four stages of their lives: childhood, adolescence, the present and finally how they imagine their image of God will develop in the future. The whole exercise is endlessly fascinating in terms of the commonalities of images produced by the students, as well as the differences, but I have always been particularly intrigued by the last section. In one way it seems to me that if a person can predict how their image or concept of God might be developing they must, in some sense, be there already, i.e., it is not a future prediction but more a projection from the present. Be that as it may, the students usually have no difficulty in completing this part of the exploration. Their future image is usually a development of, but distinct from, their present image, and tends often to be highly consistent with the descriptions of the later stages of faith development proposed by Westerhoff and especially Fowler (Fowler 1981).

I cite this example, of the future being already present to awareness in some sense, because it provides a close analogy to my own experience of embarking on a prolonged period of study with Brian Thorne. If I had been asked, when I embarked on the PhD, how I thought my understanding of humanity, divinity and spirituality might develop, I believe I would have responded with something like:

I believe that I am being led to a more radical understanding that what it means to be human and an understanding of who and what God is; that the Person-centred approach yields unique insights into what it is to be human and into human relationship; and that Christianity makes the audacious claim that divinity was capable of being fully expressed in one human being, Jesus Christ, who is the forerunner or template of redeemed humanity, and that therefore to try to understand this one human being is simultaneously to engage with understanding the divine.

That was, I believe, my anticipation of how my understanding might develop, and it has indeed turned out to be so. When I speak of 'being led' in this direction of understanding, I mean that my own journey of meaning and spirituality was already leading in this direction – the 'actualising tendency' in me at this level, if you like – but there is no doubt that I recognised in Brian Thorne a theologian who was already well travelled on this road.

The chapters

Jan Hawkins is a fitting person to start this collection. She writes closely from her experience, and indeed emphasises the importance to her of congruence between theory and practice. Being first, she is the first writer to invoke the term 'love' for the therapeutic relationship and she quotes approvingly M. Scott Peck's definition of love as 'The will to extend oneself for the purpose of nurturing one's own or another's spiritual growth'. She writes of love in action, and she writes of her *passion*:

My passion is strongly believing in freedom from oppression – by that I mean for those who have been bullied, threatened, stunted, abused, neglected and often left feeling worthless and repeating patterns set by their oppressors. My passion involves growth, development, connection, belonging, community (inner and outer), finding and removing obstacles, seeing potential and encouraging it – most of all it involves love.

She speaks out of her own experience that healing others does not require that we are completely healed ourselves, but that we are in touch with our woundedness, and healed so that we are not disabled or diminished by it. Her faith is in the self-healing at the core of the person, if only it can be encouraged and facilitated. An important part of that healing is for the person to recognize, not only their need *for* love, but their need and ability to *give* love, a believing in oneself in terms of one's lovability *and* lovingness. She poses an essential question about the courage and dedication of the therapist:

> As therapists, can we open our hearts truly to receive the love of the client when it exists, without feeling overwhelmed, or in danger of transgressing boundaries?

This leads her to explore the contretemps surrounding one of Brian Thorne's published case studies, of his work with the client Sally, and of the boundary issues which arose from it. Jan gives her personal testimony to her sense of Brian's utter trustworthiness, and also acknowledges that this case, more than any other, 'still has me on the fence'. In spite of her real cautions, there is no doubt that her faith is in a responsible but still risk-taking relationship:

> Or do we have to hide behind professional proscriptions and take what feels like a greater risk to me, and that is the risk of avoiding deeply connected relating, or what Thorne refers to as the abuse of under-involvement. What I learned, above all, from the work Thorne engaged in with Sally, was that there may be times when courage and love are fuelled by something beyond, which takes the relationship into uncharted territory, and requires trust in the self, the other and the process at the deepest possible level.

And she shares her experience of an encounter with her own therapist at a time of deep vulnerability for her, when his boundary-crossing response was deeply healing for her and not at all transgressive. She also tells of a supervision relationship where she is deeply trustful of her supervisee, Sarah's, inner process and of its external symbolization, and of a sense of accessing an energy that is more than the sum of their two personalities. (This account also resonates with the focusing approaches we will read of in later chapters of this book).

Jan concludes her chapter by exploring the emotion said to be un-convivial to Person-centered therapists: anger. She emphasises the importance of the therapist being open to receive both positive and negative aspects of the client's process, but not to encourage either at the expense of the other. Her account of a workshop she led, not of anger-management but exploring the therapeutic release of angry feelings, makes lively reading, especially where she describes the arrival of the police! In all her work she acknowledges her debt to Brian Thorne, for his example and teaching, in helping her to learn 'the reciprocal relationship between love and courage. It takes courage to love, and love gives courage'.

Mia Leijssen also invokes *love* as a crucial dimension of the therapeutic relationship, and also writes with passion. She is in no doubt of the validity of the spiritual dimension of human existence: alongside the reality of body and mind, she affirms a third perspective, that of *soul*.

> It is a bodily felt consciousness which is different from intellectual insight. The soul is not a tangible entity but a quality or a dimension of experiencing life and ourselves; it has to do with depth, value, relatedness and heart. The soul is the invisible, forming and organising principle in individual life. It is the life force which can show itself in various experiences. It is an archetype that gives direction and meaning to the individual life.

Early in her chapter she distinguishes *physical, social, psychological* and *spiritual* dimensions of human existence, but in a later section she acknowledges how interrelated are the *physical* and *spiritual*. This is explained in terms of the meeting point in consciousness between these two levels: that of the *felt sense*, (a term derived from the *focusing approach* developed initially by Eugene Gendlin, a colleague of Carl Rogers). For Mia:

> Focusing seems to bring one closer to a point of spiritual alchemy, whereby body transmutes into soul and soul into body. So the human body plays a remarkable role in developing an awareness of spirit. What is felt in the human organism increasingly leads to a broadening of the experiential field and a finding of meaning.

When we own what is really felt, our body connects to a Larger Body and shifts into a new space ... By carefully attending to certain experiences you could be led toward that gifted inner stream where the sense of being bodily alive in some Larger Process can unfold.

Mia's is the first of three chapters to explore spirituality and counselling in the context of focusing (the other two being those by Judy Moore and Alison Shoemark, and Campbell Purton respectively). Her explanation of that approach offers further fascinating insight into what this physical/spiritual awareness offers:

Focusing is the process by which we become aware of the subtle level of knowing which speaks to us through the body. The word 'body' is used here, not to indicate the 'complex machine' we can look at from the outside, but the *inwardly felt body,* the living process that grows by itself in interaction with its environment. The body that knows about what we value, about what has hurt us and how to heal it. The body that knows the right next step to bring us to a more fulfilling and rewarding life.

There has been debate in the Person-centred community about whether focusing approaches are legitimate extensions of client/person-centred theory, because they are not 'client-led' but rather 'therapist-led' to the extent that the therapist encourages the client to attend to their experiencing in this way. But Gendlin and others have responded to these questions with assertions of fidelity to the origins and spirit of Rogers' formulations:

These focusing steps I described come in client centred therapy. That is where I learnt them from, that is where I saw them and if you observe your clients, you will see that they are silent before these steps typically come. (Gendlin, 1990, p. 222)

Sanders asserts that focusing-oriented therapy is included in the Person-centred and experiential 'family' of therapies, but that the approach can permit a degree of directiveness that takes it beyond the boundaries of the family. (Sanders in Cooper, O'Hara, Schmid and Wyatt, 2007, p. 115), while Thorne suggests that much of the 'heat' has gone out of the debate, with focusing oriented practitioners bringing positive energy to the wider Person-centred community (Thorne, 1992, pp. 92–96). Thorne himself however expresses the challenge to the focusing approach at the spiritual level:

> The critical issue, however, is whether the move into focusing can be a flight for the therapist from the challenge of entering into the kind of relational depth where greater spiritual truth can be encountered. Could it be that in facilitating greater self-awareness the experiential therapists are depriving their clients of the ultimate I-Thou encounter where the liberating mystery of being is experienced? Could it be that the client ends up in touch with his or her body, attuned to the inner flow of experience, emotionally literate, and yet still alone and existentially bereft of meaning? (Thorne, 2002, p. 7)

Purton, one of the contributors to this collection, has written elsewhere that he accepts that this may be a valid observation about some ways of doing focusing, but suggests that, when the focusing oriented therapist accompanies her client sensitively, she 'stays with the client' in a perfectly Client- and Person-centred way (Purton, 2004, p. 151). In terms of the wider concern expressed by Thorne about access to a spiritual level of reality and encounter, Purton affirms the spiritual implications of Gendlin's view of reality:

> There may be ways of thinking which better accommodate the sphere of the 'paranormal', and Gendlin's philosophy, far from cutting us off from this sphere, may provide a way of thinking about it more effectively. (Purton, ibid, p. 152)

Purton further develops a view of the spiritual perspective in focusing oriented therapy in relation to emerging awareness:

> In Focusing we open ourselves to what may come. We are active in bringing our attention to a murky felt sense ... but then we wait ... and often there is a response. Word or an image 'comes', and there is a sense of release ... This opening of oneself to something else, to something unknown, clearly has something in common with spiritual practices such as prayer and meditation. (ibid, p. 230)

All four practitioners of the focusing approach in this volume relate strongly to Brian Thorne's work, and all four demonstrate in these writings the deeply spiritual values undergirding their focusing and mindfulness practice.

My own contribution to this volume: *What We are Meant to Be: Evolution as the transformation of consciousness* is an attempt to grapple with scientific and religious understandings of evolution, not just in terms of where we have come from, but in terms of where we may be going, and what it may require. I do not want to believe that our development as a life form to this point is destined to be a dead end for ourselves and the planet, and I do want to believe that the evolution of our species must have the potential to transcend the limitations of selfish competition between people and exploitation of the natural world and find a better way of cooperating with and enhancing this marvellous world and its inhabitants.

In seeking to envision how this better way can come about I draw upon three sources: Rogers' *formative* and *actualising* tendencies and his *Persons of Tomorrow*; the French Jesuit priest and palaeontologist Pierre Teilhard de Chardin and his theories of the evolution of consciousness; and the theology of the eastern orthodox churches in relation to the nature of human beings and their potential for *divinisation.* In the work of James Fowler on stages of faith development we can find a meeting place between all three.

In both Rogers' expression of a *quality of presence*, and in Thorne's description of a quality of *tenderness*, we can find some sense of what might be meant by being a *fully functioning person* at 'peak moments' in relationship and of how such experience enters upon the realm of the spiritual and of a transcendent energy. The language of divinisation suggests that the fulfilment of human development is to be found in self-giving love, Teilhard de Chardin's Omega Point, the human being fully alive.[2]

---

2. For further exploration of this last point see my paper *Self-giving and Self-actualising: Christianity and the person-centred approach* in Moore and Purton (2006), pp. 204–17.

Dave Mearns has known and worked with Brian for over 35 years. Where Brian is a committed Christian, Dave describes himself as a nihilist; indeed the first sentence of his essay here is a classic for any literary format: 'During my service of confirmation in All Saints Episcopal Church in Glasgow in 1962 I became an atheist.' He articulates the recognition he felt in terms that fit perfectly with the language used by the other writers in this collection, when describing the focusing approach: 'Such a service is intended to focus our attention on what we are saying and doing and that focusing process helped me to hear my whole self, not only my body, *talking back.*'

In his essay Dave reflects on the relationship between his faith standpoint – nihilism – and that of other faiths. He has always respected Christians of integrity and openness, in terms of who they were and how they expressed their faith, whilst being wary of those whose faith requires the conversion of others as a condition of their acceptability. He is aware that the philosophical position of nihilism can ring alarm bells for many, as if it challenges or negates their beliefs, but for Dave it is a position of the utmost existential honesty and humanism. He explains it by reference to the works of Carlos Castaneda and the concept of *controlled folly*: that is, that if there is no ultimate or absolute reason for believing in anything or making any particular choice (c.f. Purton below), then it is still open to the individual to decide to make some things matter in their lives and choose accordingly; this is their 'controlled folly': *folly* in as much as there can be no absolute justification for it, and *controlled* in as much as it is a conscious willed choice nonetheless.

In his respect for human beings, Dave fulfils for me the attitude which I have tried to express earlier in this introduction, the recognition that the human being in herself is worthy of the utmost respect and even awe, and that the goal of therapy (and religion, ideally) is to release this humanness in its fullness. Dave says it like this:

> For me I find that I do not need the hypothesis of anything beyond the person because the humanity of the individual, no matter who they are, is wondrous enough and can describe the powerful experiences people have in relationship... Yet, the reality for the person-centred therapist is that when we properly enter the

existential Self of another we find ourselves simply admiring the tenacity and the beauty of the human's survival ... We have entered the territory where nihilism and divinity meet.

In his openness to the other, Dave will endeavour to meet them where they are on their faith journey and to do so in the honesty of his own, even to the extent of being able to respond to a request to pray with one former client. He acknowledges 'the work and the pain' that have led him to his present position.

He writes that in the last decade he has wanted to challenge his readers by describing a series of clients 'they might not easily feel open towards'. He did so as a challenge to one possibility he discerned in Person-centred counselling, that of offering such a climate of empathy and acceptance that there was a 'cotton wool' relationship:

> Instead of the person-centred therapist being a congruent and full figure with whom the client could knock up against in order to feel their own firmness.

(In his chapter in this collection, Peter Schmid will echo this concern when he writes:

> Some person-centred people tend to avoid confrontation, aggression and dealing with so-called negative feelings or thoughts and I've repeatedly learned that in these cases it is the seemingly harmless image of the approach that attracted them – a result of watering down of what appeared to be too radical a challenge.)

It was partly against this background concern that Dave and Mick Cooper wrote about the power of *relational depth* (Mearns and Cooper, 2005) 'to bring the relational encounter back into attention':

> There is nothing new in relational depth other than Rogers' core conditions in powerful combination, except that it demands that the therapist does not settle for a dilution of those conditions.

It may be that Dave, with *relational depth*, and Brian, with *the quality of tenderness*, were both addressing a similar theme from their different yet related positions. This can be illustrated also by reference to their development of the concept of the self in their exploration of *configurations of self* (Mearns, 1999, p. 126; Mearns and Thorne, 2000, pp. 101–143). *Self* here is given a capital letter to denote, for Mearns, 'the existential *core* of the person' (Mearns and Thorne, ibid p. 56). For Thorne, at the heart of the person is an identity which coexists with the divine: 'at the core of our beings we find God because it is the divine nature which we share and which ultimately defines us … at the deepest level we are God.' (Mearns and Thorne, ibid p. 60). It is the ability to recognize the experience of human encounter at relational depth and yet clothe it in, respectively, secular and religious language, that distinguish Mearns and Thorne in their writings:

> We want to speak to those whose basis for existence lies in their spiritual faith and to those who may be agnostic or atheist but who place great import on the existential dimensions of the person. Our underlying question is whether these may be two languages for the same experience. (Mearns and Thorne, ibid p. 54)

Dave's own credo is amply illustrated in these pages by his descriptions of work with clients and his testimony that:

> I wanted to show how it was possible to 'reach' even such apparently difficult-to-reach clients by using nothing more, but also nothing less, than our humanity.

He ends his chapter by writing about the importance to him of maintaining the responsiveness of the counselling profession against its institutionalizing and therefore depersonalizing tendencies, and to take the wisdom of the Person-centred approach out into a wider world than that of the '10 per cent' who readily access it:

> The challenge to us is simply stated – to share our humanity and see the impact that may have on others. It is moving to find that both people of faith and those who have none can meet over this considerable relationship.

The chapter by **Judy Moore** and **Alison Shoemark** makes connections with virtually every other theme and author in this collection, either conceptually or through the acknowledgement of personal interaction and gratitude. It is one of the chapters which sets out most clearly a faith perspective, that of Buddhism, linked to focusing and Mindfulness. This last concept is treated both in its inception as 'an ancient Buddhist practice that involves total acceptance of "now", of the simple reality of the present moment', and as a contemporary therapeutic approach which again spans from the superficiality of CBT (which yet produces definite benefits) through to the deeper and more sensitive engagement of the Person-centred approach, which both authors embrace.

The conceptual and therapeutic link between Mindfulness and the Person-centred approach is found in the attitude of *acceptance*: of the present moment and all that it contains in personal process, and of *unconditional positive regard* in the Person-centred approach. Both mindfulness and focusing attend to the point of intersection in present experiencing, the 'felt sense', where consciousness and potentially change and healing can only occur:

> Experiencing which is already packaged-up in terms of familiar emotion terms is not open to change. What the focusing-oriented therapist tries to do is to help the client re-open the package.

The authors combine the Person-centred attitudes of acceptance and *relational depth* (Mearns 1997, Mearns and Cooper 2005) 'where the acceptance is not simply of the client as a person of worth but for the depths of their existential experiencing'. Both writers quote the same passage from Eliot's 'Little Gidding' as expressing so well the essence of what they are about:

> Quick now, here, now, always –
> A condition of complete simplicity
> (Costing not less than everything)
> And all shall be well and
> All manner of thing shall be well …
>   (T.S.Eliot, 'Little Gidding', Section V, *Four Quartets*)

The passage also contains a quotation – the 'all shall be well' section – from Julian of Norwich, the mediaeval mystic, local and dear to Brian Thorne. Judy Moore refers particularly to the present moment as potentially the access to the 'something more', the *orthogonal reality* (Kabat-Zinn 2005) 'in which healing occurs and where spiritual understanding may open' ('orthogonal' means 'at right angles to' as in the vertical plane in relation to the horizontal, or the spiritual in relation to the material).

Alison Shoemark's section of their joint chapter includes a case study, which not only details the progress made by the client, Theresa, but also helpfully shares Alison's internal process which, particularly in the early stages of the counselling, contained a real extent of self-doubt. As the relationship progresses we gain a clear sense that the 'work' for Alison consists in attending to her own process and whatever may be impeding her from being calmly and empathically acceptant of her client, so that then the client's actualising tendency can do the rest: a classic illustration of Person-centred therapy.

For both Judy and Alison, Mindfulness practice enables them to achieve the kind of alert and responsive state which can embody the core conditions of Person-centred therapy and can enable them to respond to their clients in ways which release them from conditioned habits of thought and emotion and to achieve a similarly mindful awareness in themselves.

If we turn now to **Campbell Purton's** essay in this volume we find a considerable contribution to the whole post-modern and empiricist debate. If other contributors to this collection have affirmed the value of human subjective experience, Purton here addresses the possibility of affirming that which is beyond intellectual definition: 'a reality which lies beyond concepts', but which is more important than conceptual understanding and which is 'central to the conception of the spiritual'. He acknowledges his debt to David Cooper's *The Measure of Things* (Cooper 2002) in developing his argument that there is a third place beyond the traditional opposition of absolute and relative truths expressed by the Modern/Post-modern debate, and which can honour the truth of both, i.e. that there is a reality beyond human consciousness which exists in itself, but that all human conceptualisations of this reality are relative and cannot claim to encompass this reality.

But if we cannot define or conceptualise this greater reality, this *Mystery* as Cooper terms it, perhaps we can acknowledge and *point towards* it, as all the mystical religions have done, and derive understandings for human life from it. The *Apophatic approach* or tradition in Christian mysticism suggests that this ultimate reality or mystery can only be approached as a 'Cloud of Unknowing' and by letting go of the desire for clarity and control. Purton quotes from various traditions to the same effect, 'that the Way which can be named is not the Way', while affirming the importance of acknowledging this further shore of understanding and seeking to approach it and learn from it by appropriate means.

If the intellect and scientific understanding and technological control have long been the mainstay of western culture, this 'third way' requires a greater humilty and openness to intuitive subjective experience. Purton has found the focusing approach to embody a helpful way to access that which is not yet known at its point of emerging into awareness and that the *felt sense* can offer an understanding both of what *is* and of what *is best* for the person in their life process. Because it involves an awareness of the totality of a given experience, it is an inclusive and holistic. It involves a cutting-edge awareness of experience as it emerges from *nothing* into *something* and in this way compares with creativity and prayer or meditation. It amounts to a dialogue between the person and themselves, between what is known and what is coming to be known: a dialogue where 'the felt sense talks back'.

Purton derives important implications from this process for ethical practice in how to live, not as a system of rules or guidelines – even though there are likely to be resonances with the major ethical systems – but in terms of access to a felt sense of what is right for the person as best they can discern in a given context. This not a system of rules imposed from outside, nor yet an internalised system of (external) rules, but as far as possible and authentic inner sense of personhood in dialogue with being.

Peter Schmid is one of the foremost philosophers of the Person-centred approach. His chapter here addresses one of the more complex and least addressed issues for that approach: the question of the nature or existence of evil and of the implications of the answer to this question for therapy. When I completed my doctoral research I was aware that this was one of the areas I had mentioned but hardly dealt with adequately. If I had had Peter's paper to hand I might have found the wherewithal to do the topic more justice!

It is not the case that Rogers held an idealised or naïve view of human nature and behaviour, and it is certainly not the case that he or other Person-centred therapists are intrinsically reluctant to engage with the 'negative' side of their clients' feelings or attitudes – or if we are, then we are failing in our stated aims – but that the emphasis in the Person-centred approach upon the actualising tendency would seem to relegate to a subsidiary category the question of the origin and nature of those attitudes and behaviours which are so destructive or abhorrent as to suggest the term 'evil'. If so, this would not seem to do justice to the prevalence in human history and into the present of such behaviours and attitudes, or to the degree of distress and antipathy they can evoke.

Peter begins with a masterly summary of the historical debate about the nature and explanation for the existence of what is termed *evil* and effectively discounts the side of the debate which would designate evil as either an objective entity or force in itself, or as a component or entity is human nature. This latter step involves the recognition that a 'genuinely person-centred and dialogical' (or relational) 'anthropology' will conceive of human nature also, not as an entity in itself but as a process and in relationship to others.

Peter quotes Dave Mearn's equivalent rejection of an objectification of evil as: 'a hypothetical construct used to describe someone whom we fear and whom we do not understand' (Mearns and Thorne, 2000, p.59), and concurs that:

> … a discussion of this question in abstract ontological categories might well be outdated, because we no longer are thinking about our experiencing and our existing in those conceptions. On the contrary we need existential answers to existential questions.

Evil then becomes understood as a consequence of nurture (or the lack of it) and of social conditioning, and of free will (which is where personal responsibility still resides). It is the wilful and conditioned refusal to be and become human in all its pain, joy and vulnerability:

Evil is to avoid personalization, to not actualize the potential of fully being and becoming a person regarding the substantial as well as the relational dimension of personhood, which means to avoid authenticity and to avoid solidarity, to avoid becoming who you are and to avoid encountering other human beings, to avoid autonomy and responsibility, to avoid sovereignty and engagement, to ignore one's possibilities and to ignore dialogue and the fundamental human We – in a word: evil is to escape from genuinely being and becoming a person.

And Peter too invokes love as the essence of personhood and relationship, and evil as the deprivation and rejection of love:

Evil is everything that opposes personal being. If the meaning of being consists in being-for-each-other, we don't talk about anything else but love. Evil is opposition to love.

Again like Dave Mearns' conclusion in his chapter here, Peter extends his analysis of loving relationship and its opposite beyond the consulting room and into the wider society and culture, and acknowledges that evil, defined and identified in these terms, can reside in groups and societies as 'structural evil'. For me, as reader, it is good to be better enabled to recognise and articulate that which should be opposed.

Conclusion

The themes we have encountered in this survey of this small volume's contents include: passion and love, soul and spirituality, presence and tenderness, healing and wholeness, honesty and integrity, focusing and mindfulness, good and evil, truth and meaning, evolution and destiny. In the unlikely event that the reader has started with this Introduction, I hope that your appetite will have been stimulated for what follows. If you are reading this at a later stage I hope you will agree with me that this collection does indeed pay worthy tribute to Brian Thorne and to the enormous significance of all these themes in his life and work – which continue! – and that each in their own way, and taken together, demonstrates the profound contribution made by the Person-centred approach to human being.

Finally, words from Lao-tse, quoted by Rogers in his final major work *A Way of Being*:

> It is as though he listened
> And such listening as his enfolds us in a silence
> In which at last we begin to hear
> What we are meant to be.
> (Rogers 1980, p. 41)

References

Cooper, DE (2002) *The Measure of Things: Humanism, humility and mystery.* Oxford: Clarendon Press.

Fowler, J (1981) *Stages of Faith: The psychology of human development and the quest for meaning.* New York: Harper & Row.

Gendlin, E (1990) The small steps of the therapy process: How they come and how to help them come. In G Lietaer, J Rombouts & R Van Balen (eds) *Client-Centered and Experiential Psychotherapy in the Nineties* (pp. 205–24). Leuven: Leuven University Press.

Kabat-Zinn, J (2005) *Coming to our Senses: Healing ourselves and the world through mindfulness.* London: Piaktus.

Leonardi, J (2006) *Self-giving and Self-actualising: Christianity and the Person-Centred Approach.* In J Moore & C Purton (eds) *Spirituality and Counselling: Experiential and theoretical perspectives* (pp. 204–17). Ross-on-Wye: PCCS Books.

Leonardi, J (2008) Partners or Adversaries: A study of Christian and person-centred approaches to spirituality, and the implications for Christian ministry and pastoral practice. PhD Thesis, University of East Anglia.

Mearns, D (1997) *Person-Centred Counselling Training.* London: Sage.

Mearns, D (1999) Person-centred therapy with configurations of self. *Counselling, 10*, 125–30.

Mearns, D & Cooper, M (2005) *Working at Relational Depth in Counselling and Psychotherapy.* London: Sage.

Mearns, D & Thorne, B (2000) *Person-Centred Therapy Today: New frontiers in theory and practice.* London: Sage.

Moore, J & Purton, C (2006) *Spirituality and Counselling: Experiential and theoretical perspectives.* Ross-on-Wye: PCCS Books.

Purton, C (2004) *Person-Centred Therapy: The focusing-oriented approach.* Basingstoke: Palgrave Macmillan.

Rogers, CR (1980) *A Way of Being.* New York: Houghton Mifflin.

Sanders, P (2007) The 'family' of person-centred and experiential therapies. In M Cooper, M O'Hara, PF Schmid & G Wyatt (eds) *The Handbook of Person-Centred Psychotherapy and Counselling.* Basingstoke: Palgrave Macmillan.

Thorne, BJ (1982) *Intimacy.* Norwich: Norvicare Occasional Paper.

Thorne, BJ (1985) *The Quality of Tenderness.* Norwich: Norwich Centre Publications.

Thorne, BJ (1991) *Person-Centred Counselling: Therapeutic and spiritual dimensions.* London: Whurr.

Thorne, BJ (1992) *Carl Rogers.* London: Sage.

Thorne, BJ (2002) *The Mystical Power of Person-Centred Therapy: Hope beyond despair.* London: Whurr.

1

Walking the Talk:
Potent therapy is a risky business

Jan Hawkins

Brian Thorne has been, and continues to be, a key influence in my personal and professional growth. Here I shall focus on how Brian's writing has always encouraged and affirmed my practice, especially in releasing the tenderness and love that I feel for many, if not all of my clients. In the current climate of 'competencies', Brian's books, lectures and the opportunities I have had to develop in his groups, have fed me and supported me in my work. I have found his writing has inspired, uplifted and challenged me. Working with him in a variety of contexts has also allowed me to learn from him as someone who is true to his word. I have never heard him speak disparagingly of anyone and have learned much from his ability to respond to challenge with openness and clarity, whilst apparently remaining rooted in his own experience.

What has especially served to influence me in my work is affirmation of my experiencing as a therapist. Early in my professional therapeutic career, I felt nervous of discussing the spiritual dimension that was so palpable in so many of my therapeutic relationships. I was nervous too, to express the love I experienced for so many of my clients and wondered if I was simply over-involved or deluding myself in witnessing the shifts and changes in people who were receiving that love through our work. Those particular dimensions of my work could be so powerful, and yet I could often yearn for the understanding of what was happening when so few would discuss those aspects of therapy. Many years on, I know that Brian's willingness to risk discussing those dimensions in his publications has drawn both positive and negative attention to himself. I am thankful that he has had the courage to do that, for my own confidence has grown as a result.

I will first highlight some of the key writings that have influenced me. I will offer examples from my own practice that I hope will illustrate the additional potency that love and spiritual connection can bring to the work.

For me, like for Val Wosket (1999), my deepest motivation and ability as a therapist rest on my capacity to love.

> I imagine I am not alone in thinking such thoughts, although I believe that many therapists may be reluctant to state publicly as Lomas did (1981, p. 7) that, 'the therapist's love for his patient often plays a significant part in healing and may even be the crucial factor'. Peck (1989, p. 91) has defined love as: 'The will to extend oneself for the purpose of nurturing one's own or another's spiritual growth'. By love in the counselling relationship I mean the ability to care deeply enough about the other person to commit myself fully and unconditionally to their process of change and development without requiring anything for myself *that might diminish the other person in return*. (author's italics) (p. 41)

So love is at the root and heart of the therapeutic endeavour for me. How I can keep my heart open. How I experience each person. How I communicate verbally and non-verbally the full range of what I am experiencing, without avoiding sharing certain feelings because of fear. In short, how I can be fully and authentically myself in the relationship, because it is the experience of the relationship that is reparative, whatever the orientation of the therapist. Well over a hundred studies and meta-analyses find a significant, consistent relationship between the therapeutic alliance and successful outcome. These findings hold across all therapy approaches studied. (Horvath and Bedi, 2002; Wampold, 2001; Martin, Garske and Davis, 2000; Krupnick, Sotsky, Simmens, Moyer, Elkin, Watkins and Pilkonis, 1996; Horvath and Symonds, 1991; Gaston, 1990). Many studies have shown that some therapists are better than others at contributing to positive client outcome. Clients describe such therapists as:

> ... more understanding and accepting, empathic, warm, and supportive. They engage in fewer negative behaviors such as blaming, ignoring or rejecting. (Lambert and Barley, 2002, p. 26)

> More than any other element to date, the therapeutic relationship
> is significantly related to positive client outcome. (Whiston and
> Sexton, 1994, p. 45)

It is through our experience and expression of acceptance, empathy,
genuineness and, where it is present, love, that the person who has
understood him- or herself to be unlovable, unacceptable and
alienated from others, begins to let go of mistaken notions of him-
or herself.

> It is my experience that those who have found healing through
> relationship with a therapist always discover that they, too, are
> loveable and capable of loving. (Thorne, 1998, p. 35)

For those people who were not met with welcome and loving
affection through infancy and childhood, it can seem impossible to
believe that anyone could love them or find them of value just
because they are who they are. The sense of insignificance and
inferiority are challenged by the genuine relationship with the
authentic therapist. Or, as Kreinheder (1980) suggests:

> If you are going to be a healer then you have to get into a
> relationship. There is a person before you, and you and that other
> person are there to relate. That means touching each other, touching
> the places in each other that are close and tender where the
> sensitivity is, where the wounds are and where the turmoil is.
> That's intimacy. When you get this close there is love. And when
> love comes, the healing comes ... Explore the full range of what
> happens when two people find intimacy. That is the greatest thing
> that is available to human beings. That is the experience a therapist
> can offer his patient, an experience that will transform the lives of
> both of you. (p. 17)

If we are to maintain an openness to experience and to the fullness
of emotional experiencing, we must continually process our own
material, our own wounds. We must trust ourselves if we are to be
potent therapists. I find support in what Brian Thorne (1996) says
of Rogers:

> Rogers tells me that I am trustworthy and desirable, despite my
> many imperfections, and that the more I can risk being fully alive
> the more I will be a transforming companion for my clients and
> for all those whose lives I touch. In short, he assures me that to be
> human is to be endowed with the spirit of life and to enjoy a
> uniqueness which paradoxically links me to my fellow human
> beings, my ancestors and the whole of the created order. (p. 1)

My passion is strongly believing in freedom from oppression – by
that I mean for those who have been bullied, threatened, stunted,
abused, neglected and often left feeling worthless and repeating
patterns set by their oppressors. My passion involves growth,
development, connection, belonging, community (inner and outer),
finding and removing obstacles, seeing potential and encouraging
it – most of all it involves love.

In my work, my purpose is to provide an environment and
relationship in which individuals are able to make the changes they
want to make in their lives. I trust that, given a relationship that is
real and genuine, that is accepting and where understanding is
communicated, people grow in trust of themselves. Part of my
purpose involves the need to continue to work on myself – I used
to think, when I was 'cured' I would work with others. I had, till
then, the erroneous notion that there was possible an end state of
curedness. The day I realised I would never be 'cured' was very
liberating, and I now prefer to think in terms of the wounded healer.
Acknowledging my own woundedness, processing and accepting
the variations of my experiencing has allowed me to come closer
to my clients in their own suffering.

> The actual process of individuation – the conscious coming to
> terms with one's own inner centre (psychic nucleus) or Self –
> generally begins with a wounding of the personality and the
> suffering that accompanies it. (Jung, 1978, p. 169)

> Fortunately the human psyche, like human bones, is strongly
> inclined towards self-healing. The psychotherapist's job, like that
> of the orthopaedic surgeon, is to provide the conditions in which
> self-healing can best take place'. (Bowlby, 1968, as cited in Steele
> and Pollock, 2000, p. 152)

> The repression of our suffering destroys our empathy for the suffering of others. (Miller, 1991, p. 10)

The idea of self-healing is at the heart of my work. But self-healing can only occur in an environment that supports it. If a person has spent their entire life experiencing abuse and denigration, their sense of who they are has been defined by other people's ideas and requirements. To make contact with their own organismic valuing process and begin the work of becoming themselves, there needs to be an environment and relationship that does not repeat the same undermining patterns – however subtly. What I mean by 'organismic valuing process' is the process by which the organism (or person) decides what is important or essential and how much this conflicts with what other people or influences think the person should be doing. My purpose as a therapist is not to make people better, but to provide the circumstances in which the person can contact their inner resources to grow. For me, the key component that allows all else to be growthful and healing is love. Of course, love need not be there for me to learn and to develop – but when I feel love is energising the relationship, then growth, development and healing seem to take on deeper and broader dimensions.

What characterises the most important relationships I have, which support me in my work is love. I am fortunate and very blessed to have relationships with my supervisor, therapist and colleagues that have love at their core. Far from making these relationships cosy and cuddly – though there may be cosy and even occasionally cuddly times, these relationships allow me to experience challenge in the most productive way. Because the energy is flowing freely between us, I am able to be open to my inner experiencing and share this, even when my thoughts and feelings are dark and confused.

The kind of love to which I am referring is defined by Rogers (1994) using the word 'agape' to describe love which:

> … respects the other person as a separate individual, and does not possess him. It is a kind of liking which has strength, and which is not demanding. (as cited in Rogers and Stevens, p. 94)

Erich Fromm (1956), however, points out that:

> ... most people see the problem of love primarily as that of *being loved* rather than that of *loving*, of one's capacity to love. (p. 9) (author's italics)

There is something about opening the heart that allows us fully to appreciate the pain and suffering of the other without being overwhelmed by it. Another aspect is not about the therapist feeling that love, but whether the therapist is able to receive the love of the client. David Brazier (1994) highlighted the fact that, for children who are abused, it is not so much that they are not loved that harms them, but that their love is not received. As therapists, can we open our hearts truly to receive the love of the client when it exists, without feeling overwhelmed, or in danger of transgressing boundaries? Can we be fully in relationship with our client without promoting an unhealthy dependency, but without either fearing what may be an essential phase of feelings of dependency in a client who has never before been able to depend upon another person?

> Being able to give care sensitively and to receive care gratefully is far more difficult than it might seem. (Nelson, 2005, p. 105)

When thinking of the risk of acting from conviction, I am drawn back again to something I learned early in my training. I kept hearing of a prominent therapist whose work was being described with contempt and ridicule. I am often drawn, when hearing such negative commentary, to find out for myself what all the fuss is about. So I found the paper in question and read it. Its title was *Beyond the Core Conditions* (1987) and was written by Brian Thorne, who then, as now, is a prominent therapist and writer in the Person-centred tradition. For someone in that position to take such a risk inspires admiration in me. When I read *Beyond the Core Conditions,* I sat well and truly on the fence. I could not imagine myself having the courage to go as far as Thorne did in his relationship with Sally.

Essentially the paper describes a therapeutic relationship with a woman called Sally who was suffering from a deep disconnection from herself and her husband with whom she initially came into therapy. It became clear that Sally needed to work in therapy on her own before any useful couples work could begin. They agreed that Sally would work individually and that her husband would join them from time to time to explore how things were going for them as a couple in the light of that work. At all times the work they did was transparent. The aspect of the work that caused controversy was that Sally and Brian had a session in which they were naked together. This was prompted by Sally's total contempt and dislike for her own body and her deep conviction that she could not be desirable. Further, she was frightened of being in the presence of a naked man. The trust they had built up allowed, and Thorne would say demanded, this risk to be taken. That Sally could be naked and acceptable, as well as being in the presence of a naked man, who accepted his own body and was not going to sexualise the relationship, was deeply healing and transformative for her. I am not advocating this as a technique. This remains the only piece of writing in the therapeutic literature I have read which still has me on the fence. Over the years, I have come to know Brian Thorne personally, and find him to be as trustworthy as a person could be. But he took an incredible risk not only in his relationship with Sally, but also in publicly exploring it. I want to give here his words on this:

> Sally's uncompromising faith in me forced me to face myself in two fundamental ways. First, she made me question how much I really valued the particular approach to therapy which I professed to practise. In effect, she incited in me a commitment to the basic tenets of person-centred therapy which surpassed in depth and tenacity any previous allegiance on my part. Secondly, she demanded my integrity. I was compelled to face the complete range of my beliefs and feelings about myself, the world and the human race, and when I discovered apparent contradictions, to search for some kind of resolution. Whatever safety I might have had in the therapist role was ruthlessly stripped away by Sally's consuming faith in my genuineness. She compelled me to be honest. I suggest that it might be no bad thing if every therapist asked two questions of himself or herself every year or so: 1. What would it mean if I *really* practised the therapy I profess? 2. What do I believe about my own nature, the human race of which

> I am a part and the world in which I live? And then in the light of
> the answers, to re-examine his or her professional activities.
> (Thorne, 1987 in Dryden, 1987, p. 71) (author's italics)

Thorne received and still receives masses of letters from therapists
and others, for whom *Beyond the Core Conditions* has brought
hope of true companionship and healing, of real and genuine
connectedness. Yet he has also often profoundly regretted publishing
it.

> There are those who have taken the opportunity to accuse me of
> irresponsibility, of arrogance, of immorality, of blindness, of self-
> delusion and – most powerfully of all – of giving license to others
> to trespass across all the boundaries in the therapeutic relationship.
> (1996, p. 7)

He was investigated by the BAC (British Association for
Counselling, now BACP) in order to find out whether or not there
was the possibility that his writing might have brought the
profession into disrepute. Though the investigation did not go
beyond the initial stages, Brian was asked, and agreed, to make it
clear in subsequent reprintings of the chapter that since the
publication of the BAC's Code of Ethics and Practice, work of the
kind described in that chapter would be deemed contrary to the
code as currently interpreted. He realised that if his work with Sally
had not been completed before 1984, his position in the eyes of the
profession may have been much more perilous. Brian still does not
know whether going ahead and publishing:

> ... was a courageous act or whether it was the result of foolish
> naiveté which would predictably lead to misunderstanding,
> confusion and in some quarters outright condemnation. (ibid., p. 8)

He is convinced still that without his willingness to take those risks
to be completely real in the existential encounter with Sally, the
deep healing which occurred in her would not have happened. The
cost of publicly exploring this experience, though, has led him to
regret at times its publication.

If only I had kept quiet my reputation would have remained unblemished and I should have been spared the vicious letters in the morning post or the unexpected barbs at professional meetings or in the therapy literature. (ibid. p. 8)

Yalom (1980) recognises this dilemma in which a potent therapist may find him- or herself:

During the course of effective psychotherapy the therapist frequently reaches out to the patient in a human and deeply personal manner. Though this reaching out is often a critical event in therapy, it resides outside the official ideological doctrine; it is generally not reported in psychiatric literature (usually because of shame or fear of censure) nor is it taught to students (both because it lies outside of normal theory and because it might encourage 'excesses'). (p. 402)

Yalom is highlighting the riskiness of *real* connection and the willingness to know and be known at depth in the therapeutic relationship. Further, he points to the vulnerability of the therapist to judgement within their own particular tradition of therapy, as well as a general lack of trust in the integrity of practitioners. This means that all traditions of counselling/therapy can imply that theory or a particular set of 'rules' are more important than the unique event in the single relationship. He also illuminates the reasons why so few of the deeper, unique interventions which release so much healing, are not reported. Brian Thorne was not only willing to take the risk in the therapeutic relationship he had with Sally, but by publishing openly what had been a powerful healing experience, he had put himself in danger of misunderstanding at best and committing professional suicide at worst. Yet without the courage and transparency of practitioners who have been open to the fullness and depth of relating, how can others learn? Potent therapy is about trusting in one's own integrity *and* that of the client, sometimes entering a 'zone' where the only healing thing to do is to let go of fear of judgement and *connect*. In my experience, when these 'zone' moments arise, I have a feeling of fluidity. Somehow my client's energy and my own are interwoven and I *know* I can trust what is happening, because I somehow also feel in every pore of my being that my client is also trusting the experience. As if we both have let go temporarily of a need to make logical or rational sense and plunge together into what it happening. For me it can feel as though we are two dolphins, swimming together, plunging into the depths of my client's sea and re-emerging parallel with each other. At these times there is a sense of energies released, pain unblocked, of movement. My sense is that Brian Thorne and Sally were entering these kinds of zones. Without Brian taking the risk of writing about it, my own development as a therapist would have been so much lonelier and probably more fearful. There are so many moments in therapy when one is faced with the potential for connection and for healing as a result:

> Crying is above all a relationship behaviour, a way to help us get close and not simply a vehicle for emotional expression or release. We do not cry because we need to get *rid* of pain, but because we need connection with our caregivers – literal, internal, fantasised, or symbolic – in order to accept and heal from our pain and grief. Crying is not about what we let *out* but whom we let *in*. (Nelson, 2005, p. 6) (author's italics)

There is something profoundly important in the willingness to be brave, to have courage, to know that we are in unknown terrain, but are there in an existential encounter which has the potential for the deepest of healing. Do we have the courage to be fully present, utterly and authentically ourselves? Are we able to enter into the intimacy of the existential encounter, aware of our own inner flow at the same time as being in the deepest connection with the flow of our client? Or do we have to hide behind professional proscriptions and take what feels like a greater risk to me, and that is the risk of avoiding deeply connected relating, or what Thorne refers to as the abuse of under-involvement. What I learned, above all, from the work Thorne engaged in with Sally, was that there may be times when courage and love are fuelled by something beyond, which takes the relationship into uncharted territory, and requires trust in the self, the other and the process at the deepest possible level.

Of course, what is required is integrity and trust in ourselves if we are to walk our talk – and part of that trust is to ensure we have a potent supervisory relationship. Without a courageous supervisor, we could be arrogantly self-deceptive in our thinking about the risks we take. The supervisory relationship needs to be safe enough, robust enough, supportive enough and developmental enough for the challenge of exploring all the edges of therapeutic practice. This important relationship is essential so that responsible and ethical practice is monitored, but not constrained. In supervision and his/her own personal therapy, or other self care strategies, the therapist is continually developing his/her capacity to connect deeply with him/herself and others. Person-centred therapy requires that I use my whole self and that I take care of myself because I cannot rely on techniques or tools in my work with my clients. It requires continual development and embodiment of the core attitudinal qualities of empathy, congruence and unconditional positive regard. And whilst these 'core conditions', as they are often referred to, have been diluted in some training courses to mean *doing* empathy rather than *being* empathic, there is no possibility of relating at depth unless the therapist is *experiencing* the blend of these attitudinal qualities. Communicating that experiencing allows the client to truly feel known, heard and often loved. It feels to me that it is through the experiencing of the core attitudinal qualities that the quality of tenderness is released.

> What does it mean for a person to possess the quality of tenderness in all its fullness? In the first place, it is a quality which irradiates the total person – it is evident in the voice, the eyes, the hands, the thoughts, the feelings, the beliefs, the moral stance, the attitude to things animate and inanimate, seen and unseen. Secondly, it communicates through its responsive vulnerability that suffering and healing are interwoven. Thirdly, it demonstrates a preparedness and ability to move between the worlds of the physical, the emotional, the cognitive and the mystical without strain. Fourthly, it is without shame because it is experienced as the joyful embracing of the desire to love and is therefore a law unto itself. Fifthly, it is a quality which transcends the male and female but is nevertheless nourished by the attraction of the one for the other in the quest for wholeness.

It will be evident that so breath-taking a quality is rare. What is more no one person can hope to embody it more than fleetingly and intermittently, for to be irradiated by it is to achieve a level of humanness which belongs to the future and not to now. (Thorne, 2004, p. 9)

My hunch is that with some of my clients it is in a moment of tenderness that I am able to extend to them that welcome to the world which they never received at birth. It is as if they have been waiting all their lives for the completion of the liberating paradox. (ibid., pp. 12–13)

In my own therapy, I know that the deepest healing has happened when my therapist has taken risks. When his willingness to express his tenderness and connection to me has made him vulnerable to misunderstanding and potential complaint. One such event in particular stands out as it could so easily have put him in danger of a complaint. At the time I was dealing with some extremely painful traumatic material. The depersonalisation I experienced involved the sensation of my face melting like wax from my skull, leaving my face exposed as ugly and revolting. I was describing that experience at the same time as having it (dissociation is an amazing process), fully expecting my therapist to display disgust and recoil. Instead, he leaned forward and kissed my cheek. He kissed the cheek that I experienced as melting in disgusting globules from my bones. Though in a very dissociated state, that kiss registered and, some time later, I checked if it had actually happened. Somehow it was hard for me to believe. It was an extraordinarily deep and healing experience. I cannot imagine any words he might have said or any other action that would have been so deeply full of love, tenderness, acceptance and healing. Yet the risk he took was that I might perceive it otherwise. I give this example because it had such a profound impact on me. The additional gift within it was the implicit trust he had in me to know what that kiss meant. He was willing to reach out from his soul, beyond what we would normally expect of a therapist because in that moment, those circumstances and that unique relationship, it was the only healing thing to do. He was able to trust and reach out from his own soul to mine, such that the healing could occur at a spiritual level, deeper than words could ever convey.

This reminds me of Brian Thorne's courage in his relationship with Sally.

> The chief danger in life is that you may take too many precautions. (Alfred Adler, cited in Roth and Aberson, 2006, p. 111)

> Every blade of grass has its Angel that bends over it and whispers, 'Grow, Grow'. (The Talmud, as cited in Cameron, 1994, p. 3)

As therapists we are learning – continually learning. If we stay within the safety of technique and professional distance, we can probably do no harm, and sometimes we may do a lot of good. Having spent years learning and training and experiencing in order to work as therapists, there will have been many times when we have felt we have fallen short of the ideals of our own particular school of thought. The danger then is that we become discouraged, and stay in the safety of our own particular therapeutic comfort zone. Potent therapy is a risky business. It relies not on technique, nor on great intellectual insight, but on connection, on courage and on many mistakes along the way. To be a companion who is alive in the process of healing, we have to live, we have to be alive to living and have the courage to makes mistakes. The times when I have found myself going to the edge have been those where something greater than my client and I seems present. Something has changed in the space between us and we are transported into another realm where there is nothing to do than follow the flow and trust in the process. Those are the times when the deepest healing seems to take place. Those are the times when all I can say to myself afterwards is that I had to 'trust in the process'.

> The therapist's task is thus formidable for he or she has somehow to rekindle hope in the client's heart and that is impossible without the rediscovery of trust … Psychological skills, therapeutic insights, sophisticated medication may all have their part to play in the process of healing but, as St. Paul put it in another context, without love they are likely in the end to profit nothing. (Thorne, 1998, p. 108)

> *Love is the active concern for the life and the growth of that which we love* … Beyond the element of giving, the active character of

love ... always implies certain basic elements, common to all forms
of love. These are *care, responsibility, respect and knowledge.*
(Fromm, 1957, p. 28) (author's italics)

An incredible gift of healing is possessed by many persons if only
they feel free to give it. (Rogers, 1970, p. 32)

From my own experience, here is another case-example where 'trust
was put in the process'. Sarah is a palliative care nurse specialist,
who meets with me for supervision on a fortnightly basis. Although
she is not a counsellor, Sarah sees the person-to-person aspect of
her work as more important than her specialist clinical knowledge
and advice on palliative care. She sought supervision to ensure
that she has space to process the painful issues she experiences in
her work and to allow herself to develop her skills in coming
alongside patients in their dying.

Sarah is my only supervisee who is not working as a
counsellor, yet her processing of her relationships with her patients
and their families are the focus of our work, in the same way as
other supervisees focus on their relationships with their clients.
Though we may, at times, discuss clinical dilemmas, these are in
the context of Sarah's desire to relate at depth to her patient, rather
than simply advise, prescribe and move on. The work we do
together often has a spiritual quality as we explore together
sometimes very complicated issues that arise for people as they
face their imminent death. For a nurse to take the time to allow
her patient to explore their fears, their concerns and their varying
spiritual and/or religious needs, whilst also balancing their clinical
needs, seems to me a formidable and sometimes overwhelming
prospect. That Sarah has managed to maintain her passion and
conviction over the years that I have been working with her, leaves
me with awe.

In one session Sarah wanted to acknowledge the deaths of
seven patients in the previous week. She was unsure how she
wanted to acknowledge these deaths and we sat for some moments
in silence considering this. She had a sense of desire for some
sort of ritual, but it was hard to decide what might be possible or
acceptable in, what was then, our fairly new relationship, this
being only our fourth session. I was aware of a sense of reverence

in myself, which I realised was not only about those people who had died in the last week, but also about my sense of Sarah as someone whose nursing went beyond the practical advising on or administering painkilling and comfort-promoting drugs. In allowing myself fully to experience that reverence, I felt she and I were connecting in something of an altered state of consciousness. A different energy was present in the room and in the space between us. Staying in the silence, I have learned, is very important to Sarah, but this was early in our relationship when I was just getting to know her. So the power of this particular silence was almost of a throbbing nature.

Some moments elapsed before she mentioned that being in the open seemed important and I invited her to go into the garden. Outside Sarah chose flowers or sprigs of foliage for each of her patients who had died that week. There followed a simple act of remembering each person by name. She talked very briefly about them all, including one man who really had nobody, very few visits from family, left to die alone. Another who wanted 'a good piss-up, and to die in my own bed', which Sarah had been able to facilitate so that he could have the death he wanted. For her, listening to the wishes of her patients and doing her utmost to facilitate them in having the death they want is a key aspect of her approach to her work. She acknowledged that some of the seven she knew well, whilst others she had hardly met. I reflected that she had connected with each, if only momentarily in some cases, and her desire was to acknowledge their importance to her, which she did. As she spoke of each, the selected flower or piece of foliage was placed into a small vase I had brought out with us. When we had finished, and she felt ready, she decided that the vase with those flowers should be left in the garden. We placed it safely among some pots, where I knew it would not be disturbed.

I gave a prayer of thanks after Sarah had left, as her prizing of her patients touched me deeply, and showed me in another person, what I so often feel. Simple acts of love are the most profound to me. Sarah's care and attention to each of those patients in that session ensured that none of them had passed unnoticed from this world. Even the man, who had nobody, had somebody who cared enough to bring him to the garden and give him a sprig of foliage and thought.

I would now like to counter – and illustrate with a case-example – one of the criticisms levelled against the Person-centred approach, which was voiced by a trainee counsellor whom I supervise, 'Person-centred counsellors are not able to deal with angry people, are they?'

My own sense is that the Person-centred approach can only be as potent as the person practising it. That is to say, if the person of the therapist is so caught up in the positive potential, the 'actualising tendency', then they may find it difficult to be with the more destructive aspects of self that co-exist in those who seek to develop themselves and grow. If we are not open to all aspects of the person, including the 'not for growth' tendency, or what Jung refers to as 'the shadow', then we are not able to be fully with another. If we are lost in a desire to experience or promote only 'positive' feelings, we are unlikely to be able to meet some of our clients in the deepest, most shameful parts of their being.

In my early years as a therapist, I feared that I might block people in their expression of anger, as I was continually being prodded to be angry about experiences I had endured in my life. Well meaning therapists, who desired my best development I'm sure, were convinced that I was denying my anger, or blocking it from my awareness, being unable themselves to recognise that my feelings went deeper than anger. For some years, in my own therapy I trusted more in what therapists thought I should feel, than in what I actually felt for myself. A gradual dawning of awareness allowed me to see that my earliest experiences, which might naturally have induced expressions of rage, had actually taught me something different.

As Rogers points out, conditions of worth imposed in our earliest days teach us to deny or distort our organismic needs to try to meet the needs and requirements of our caregivers. In my case, screaming and crying were either met with complete indifference, abandonment (being left in the house alone for many hours) or violence. As a baby, when needs are not met, rage gives way to despair. Because of this, in facing experiences that others thought I ought to be angry about, all I felt was hurt and despair. My concern as a therapist then was, would I be able to support people who did feel and need to express anger, when I was not an easily-angered person myself, so might have less empathy with anger.

Because of this concern I began to explore anger from an academic viewpoint, reading all I could about it and attending anger workshops to learn more about it. From there, I included anger-management in the workshops I offered and came to realise that I was not blocking others' anger, but was actually capable of facilitating the expression of anger in people who feared it in themselves, due to uncontrollable explosions in them at times. I have written elsewhere (Hawkins, 1997) of my concerns about how the expression of anger is sanctioned by some forms of therapy and some therapists, regardless of the impact this has on the recipient of those angry feelings. My anger workshops and weekly courses have allowed people to come together to focus on what their own and others' anger means to them. Here I want to describe one particular session, the outcomes of which could never have been predicted or timed, but which had an unusually healing effect on participants.

A group with whom I had been working for several sessions, had talked of desperate physical needs to rid themselves of tightly contained anger that some felt could never be expressed. Others had experienced uncontrolled raging which left them feeling ashamed of their behaviour, having hurt people they cared about. As the need for physical expression was explored, a shared fantasy arose, of smashing things.

Something about the noise and destruction this suggested seemed, to some in the group, to have the potential to release them from their darker destructive feelings, for which no words could be found. There was a sense of hopelessness that this would ever be possible, but on working out how it could be made feasible as a positive experience, a plan arose which involved checking with the centre we used – whether or not there was a wall somewhere outside against which things could be smashed. The manager of the centre, who is usually completely 'unphasable' by my efforts to facilitate unusual needs for groups with whom I work, simply pointed to a wall outside and said: 'What about that?'

On the appointed evening, we informed the other group using the centre that evening that there might be some noise outside, and not to worry. The group had brought in some crockery and we began that session as always, checking in how each member was. There was much discussion about the planned event. Some had reflected on the previous week's session and decided that physical release was not for them. In fact, this decision for some of them was in recognition that they often did use physical means of expressing their anger and did not want to go that route any more. The group explored how the session would be and my role was to facilitate this and to ensure that everybody felt heard. The group divided themselves almost in half, with half staying inside to explore together what hearing the exercise outside felt like and to consider their own desire to articulate their anger through calmer means. As that was their shared goal at that time I was to facilitate the half of the group who went outside.

When outside, we considered together what each person would like from the others whilst expressing their anger. I had asked that there be a commitment to safety, not only for each other, but also for the self. Many of the participants had experienced self-harm and I wanted to encourage them to value themselves in this process.

Each person decided how they wanted to use the wall and the crockery and there was much release. The group supported and encouraged each person as some projected images of abusers onto the wall, then smashed plates at them, letting go of fury that had been pushed down for years. Others let go the missile by way of symbolically throwing away anger about a particular event. There were many variations. At the end, there was release, many tears had been shed, much shouting had been done, and the group were together feeling stronger. It was time for coffee. On this one occasion, it seemed important that, this one time, they should not have to clear up the mess made by their expressions of anger, no hint of punishment, but simply acceptance of various feelings and of the mess; those feelings were now in pieces, finished, to be walked away from. I needed to clean up the broken material for the safety of the centre and began this during coffee time. It was during this clean-up process that two Police cars suddenly appeared and several officers jumped out, looking at me.

Policeman: *We got reports of smashing noises.*

Me: (Rather embarrassed): *Yes, it was my anger-management group.*

Policeman: *There were reports of screaming too.*

Me: (Feelings more ridiculous by the minute): *Yes, they were expressing their feelings.*

Policeman: (Talking to his lapel microphone): *It's all right Guv, it's an anger-management course.*

For the participants of the course, this unplanned denouement gave an unexpected dimension to their release work, as well as bringing together the two halves of the group with much humour. Much rich material came from all that was symbolically played out during that session. I am always amazed by the healing that occurs when I can listen carefully to people and facilitate their own creativity, giving permission for them to give themselves permission to make happen what feels intuitively necessary for them, even though it is completely outside my own frame of reference. Trust in deep intuition can take one into unusual situations, where feared destructive impulses give way to inner freedom.

There are risks that I sometimes take in my work. Often my boldness takes me by surprise and I would doubt what I do, indeed not have taken these risks which have brought about understanding and healing, had I not learned the reciprocal relationship between love and courage. It takes courage to love and love gives courage. This was taught me to a large extent by my mentor. Reading and working alongside Brian Thorne has been a continually affirming and challenging process. Most importantly, I have admired his courage to remain true to himself, sometimes in the face of open hostility in the press or in public lectures. Brian's articulation of those essential aspects of the spiritual dimension in therapeutic relationships has supported me in my own professional life and validated for me the experience I have had in encounter with all my clients, including those who have severe learning disabilities and therefore cannot verbalise their own struggles and concerns. I have had to trust that the love, tenderness and attention I can offer will reach them in a particular way in the time we spend together.

The words of W.H. Auden (1940) encapsulate perfectly love's imperative:

We must love one another or die. (p. 105)

References

Auden, WH (2007) September 1, 1939. In: *Another Time.* (pp. 103–6) London: Faber & Faber Ltd. (First Published 1940).

Bowlby, J (1968) A psychiatric study of parents who abuse infants and small children. In: BF Steele and CB Pollock (eds) *Secure Base: Clinical applications of attachment* (2000). London: Routledge.

Brazier, D (1994) Beyond Carl Rogers. In: T. Merry (ed) (2000) *The BAPCA Reader.* Ross-on-Wye: PCCS Books. (First published in *Person-Centred Practice*, *2*(1), 5–10)

Brazier, D (2000) Beyond Carl Rogers. In: T Merry (ed) *The BAPCA Reader.* Ross-on-Wye: PCCS Books. (First published in *Person-Centred Practice*, 2000, 2(1), 97–102.

Cameron, J (1994) *The Artist's Way: A spiritual path to higher creativity.* London: Souvenir Press.

Fromm, E (1957) *The Art of Loving.* London, ON: Mandala Books.

Gaston, L (1990) The concept of the alliance and its role in psychotherapy: Theoretical and empirical considerations. *Psychotherapy,* 27, 143–53.

Hawkins, J (1997) A Choice Model for Anger Expression: Encouraging Responsibility. *Changes: An International Journal of Psychology and Psychotherapy, VOL NO??* (3), PAGE RANGE.

Horvath, AO & Symonds, BE (1991) Relation between working alliance and outcome in psychotherapy: A meta-analysis. *Journal of Counselling Psychology, 38,* 139–49.

Horvath AO & Bedi, RP (2002) The alliance. In JC Norcross (ed) *Psychotherapy Relationships That Work* (pp. 37–69). New York: Oxford University Press.

Jung, C (1978) *Man and His Symbols.* London: Picador Edition, Pan Books.

Kreinheder, A (1980) The healing power of illness. *Psychological Perspectives, 11*(1), 9–18.

Krupnick, JL, Sotsky, SM, Simmens, A, Moyer, J, Elkin, I, Watkins, J & Pilkonis, PA (1996) The role of the alliance in psychotherapy and pharmacotherapy outcome: Findings in the National Institute of Mental Health Treatment of Depression Collaborative Research Program. *Journal of Consulting and Clinical Psychology, 64,* 532–9.

Lambert, MJ & Barley, DE (2002) Research summary on the therapeutic relationship and psychiatric outcome. In: JC Norcross (ed) *Psychotherapy Relationships That Work.* (pp. 17–32). New York: Oxford University Press.

Martin, DJ, Garske, JP & Davis, MK (2000) Relation of the therapeutic alliance with outcome and other variables: A meta-analytic review. *Journal of Consulting and Clinical Psychology, 68*, 438–50.

Miller, A (1991) *Banished Knowledge*. London: Virago.

Nelson, JK (2005) *Seeing Through Tears: Crying and attachment*. London: Routledge.

Peck, MS (1989) *The Road Less Travelled*. London: Century Hutchinson. (First published in 1978).

Rogers, CR (1961) *On Becoming a Person*. Boston: Houghton Mifflin.

Rogers, CR (1970) *On Encounter Groups*. New York: Harper and Row.

Rogers, CR (1994) The interpersonal relationship: The core of guidance. In: CR Rogers & B Stevens. *Person to Person: The problem of being human.* London: Souvenir Press (First published in 1967).

Roth, B, Roth, H & Aberson, T (2006) *Compelling Conversations: Questions and quotations on timeless topics*. Charleston: BookSurge.

Thorne, B (1987) Beyond the core conditions. In: W Dryden (ed) *Key Cases in Psychotherapy*. London: Croom.

Thorne, B (1996) The cost of transparency. A lecture given to the Annual General Meeting of the British Association for the Person-Centred Approach. University of East Anglia, Norwich, 15th June 1996.

Thorne, B (1998) *Person-Centred Counselling and Christian Spirituality: The secular and the holy*. London: Whurr Publishers.

Thorne, B (2004) *The Quality of Tenderness*. Revised text. A Norwich Centre Occasional Publication.

Wampold, BE (2001) *The Great Psychotherapy Debate*. Mahwah, NJ: Lawrence Erlbaum Associates.

Whiston, SC & Sexton, TL (1994) The status of the counselling relationship: An empirical review, theoretical implications and research directions. *The Counseling Psychologist, 22*, 6–78.

Wosket, V (1999) *The Therapeutic Use of Self: Counselling practice, research and supervision*. London: Routledge.

Yalom, I.D. (1980) *Existential Psychotherapy*. New York: Basic Books.

2

Caring for the Soul as the Keystone in Health Care

Mia Leijssen

On the one hand, the soul is tangible as a sort of *inner compass*, a bodily felt *inspiration*. On the other hand that *inward*-oriented movement is inseparably linked to an *outward*-oriented movement of *connectedness* with something that transcends the person. The person can experience the soul as an element of the divine living at the centre of the human personality.

The soul expresses itself through our capacity for giving and receiving love. People need sometimes a counselling relationship to discover this healing potential and to open spiritual generosity. Carl Rogers formulated the critical ingredients of a healing relationship: acceptance, empathy and congruence. Later in his therapeutic career he discovered *'presence'*. In this state a person makes connection with a higher source of wisdom, a symbol of Absolute Presence.

The experience of the soul is a bodily felt consciousness. Gendlin described this bodily awareness process that transcends what is known on the levels of behaviour, emotion and cognition, and brings meaning from a new level. The felt sensing body is connected to the whole universe and brings a connection with Spirit, the Mystery that works beyond our wills, our techniques, and our understanding. The ultimate healing process involves a connection between and beyond the counsellor/ client relationship, including the possibility of a Divine Intervention.

This chapter is an adaptation of Leijssen's Keynote Address at the International Conference on Spirituality in Health Care. India, October 2009.

Dimensions of human existence

Through my work as a psychotherapist and through different experiences in my personal and family life, the spiritual dimension has become the core of my work and life. In this article, in honour of Brian Thorne, I'll articulate how a counselling process can contribute to discovering the soul and why caring for the soul is crucial for healing and transformation.

Human beings seem to develop from a preoccupation with physical survival, through learning how to live with others and being in a group, to discovering individuality, and ultimately to deepening the spiritual (van Deurzen, 1997). These four dimensions of human existence: the physical, social, psychological and spiritual, are echoed in many developmental theories and in different faith traditions. They provide a useful grid for mapping human concerns: from survival to comfort and health, from recognition to belonging and love, from autonomy to identity and freedom, from finding meaning in life to truth and wisdom.

In any particular culture, or for one individual, one of these dimensions is particularly salient. But change in any domain can lead to knock-on changes in the others. For example, a person who becomes paralysed after a brain damage may face a destiny of being dependent on others and losing his autonomy. The resulting crisis can trigger the spiritual dimension. A healing process includes the physical, social and psychological dimensions over time, while the ultimate healing seems to come from an opening up to the spiritual dimension, a resource beyond that of our own will, a self transcendent source. The character of health care can be deepened and enriched, even transformed, when the spiritual dimension is addressed in the treatment.

Evoking the spiritual dimension

Before continuing to address the spiritual dimension in health care, I'll offer a few *questions* to capture a little bit of the salience of spirituality in one's personal life. The questions hint at resources, destinations, struggles and transformations in one's life and the possibility of a deeper dimension.

What gives you peace or comfort; strength or courage in your life?

For what are you deeply grateful?

What makes you feel joyful?

What are you striving for in your life?

How would you like people to remember you when you are gone?

Who or what do you put your faith and hope in?

To whom, or what, do you most freely express love?

When have you felt most deeply and fully alive?

What are the experiences which changed your life?

What are moments which you found extremely difficult or which you regret?

What would you like to be able to let go of in your life?

What gives you the feeling that you are making the best of life?

These are questions adapted from Pargament (2007), and Griffith and Griffith (2002). With similar questions they elicit clients' spiritual stories, or guide therapists in the telling of their autobiographies in order to explore what someone's sensitivities are on the level of religion. The questions do not refer directly to higher powers, religious institutions or religious practices. Instead they make use of psychological language, psychologically meaningful concepts carrying emotionally powerful connotations. This way of working goes hand in hand with the use of Positive psychology (Snyder and Lopez, 2001). Positive psychology reflects a change in approaching health. Taking seriously the contributions of virtues and strengths alongside traumas and vulnerability, is a paradigmatic shift. However, the questions given above dig deeper than is usually the goal in Positive psychology. These questions evoke the spiritual dimension, because they point to people's soul.

The Soul

Commonly, in the literature it is suggested that body, mind and soul are different orders of reality, each with its own perspective (Elkins, 2005). The body's reality consists of sensations and emotions, whereas that of the mind consists of thoughts, feelings and desires. Our experience is more than a combination of these, however, so that we need to distinguish a third perspective, that of the soul. The soul is about meaning in life, what we do with our physical and mental states, what they mean to us in our deepest subjectivity. We use body and mind as tools for living, but the soul is about *how* we live, what it is like for us to live, and about what really matters to us. It is a bodily felt consciousness which is different from intellectual insight. The soul is not a tangible entity but a quality or a dimension of experiencing life and ourselves; it has to do with depth, value, relatedness and heart.

The soul is the invisible, forming and organising principle in individual life. It is the life force which can show itself in various experiences. It is an archetype that gives direction and meaning to the individual life. It transcends the limited self through the experience of belonging to a larger process. So, on the one hand, the soul is tangible as a sort of *inner compass*, a bodily felt *inspiration*. On the other hand that *inward*-oriented movement is inseparably linked to an *outward*-oriented movement of *connectedness* with something that transcends the person. These movements go together like the process of breathing in and breathing out.

The additional value of the concept 'soul' compared to, for instance, the concept of 'person' is that the soul is bound to a person as well as being transpersonal. It does not stop at the boundaries of the person; it transcends the person. It points to the mystic dimension of human experience. Mysticism is a process through which a connectedness to a larger process is experienced. The person can experience the soul as an element of the divine living at the centre of the human personality.

This element of the divine can express itself through our thinking, our feelings, our actions, and in silence where we can arrive at a deeper level of consciousness. These are four different paths of spirituality: the path of thinking, the path of feeling, the path of actions and the path of silence. An individual might have a preference for some specific path(s) to transcend the limited self.

The self-transcendent experience is not a wandering condition; it is an experience which is specially grounded in our earthly existence and in what can be bodily felt. Being mindful to what presents itself in the here and now improves the opportunity for a person to reach the domain of the soul. The soul can be experienced as a bodily felt vibration. This immediate experience can show itself in the form of joy, poignancy, gratitude, astonishment, connection, but also as remorse, guilt, regret, disappointment. For example, sadness or anger can hint at sacred loss or violation. And most of all, the soul expresses itself through our capacity for giving and receiving love (Thorne, 2006). Love is the key to accessing the healing potential and to open spiritual generosity.

Counselling as building a relationship, making connection

How can a counselling process provide the conditions for evoking the spiritual dimension? Carl Rogers (1961) formulated the critical ingredients of a healing relationship: acceptance, empathy and congruence. These attitudes belong to the most evidence-based ingredients of every therapeutic approach. Science recognizes thus what in spiritual traditions is emphasized as the importance of love, compassion, truth. Carl Rogers was a master in making explicit the conditions for healing relationships. Later in his life he became more and more intrigued by the sacred moments which occasionally occurred in the therapeutic encounter. Martin Buber (1970), the philosopher who distinguished between two types of relationship: I–it and I–Thou, emphasized that people can respond to any aspect of life as a 'Thou'. In this kind of I–Thou relationship people come close to an encounter with the divine. In a dialogue with the theologian Paul Tillich, Carl Rogers admitted: 'I feel at times when I'm really being helpful to a client of mine … there is something approximating an I-Thou relationship between us, then I feel as though I am somehow in tune with the forces of the universe or that forces are operating through me in regard to this helping relationship' (Rogers, 1989, p.74).

By caring for patients, therapists may experience themselves as participating in a sacred activity. In my experience the larger field of the transpersonal is palpable in the room in those moments of profound meeting when client and therapist are expressing their soul. When we say that the relationship heals, this is another way of expressing that there is soul-to-soul contact.

The immediate encounter with the sacred is more than a matter of the mind; it is deeply bodily felt and hard to put it into words (Leijssen, 2008). Rogers discovered that when a person truly listens to another the process of growth and development is set free. By providing empathy, respect, caring, acceptance, honesty... the therapist nurtures the client's soul. One of the effects of these attitudes is that the client can bring more awareness to the ongoing experiencing process. Other effects are that the client can relive traumatic events in a more benevolent context and reconstruct the story of his/her life. The relationship thus defines how and what is being experienced. Later in his therapeutic career Rogers (1980) discovered '*presence*'. To quote him:

> I find that when I am closest to my inner, intuitive self, when I am somehow in touch with the unknown in me, when perhaps I am in a slightly altered state of consciousness, then whatever I do seems to be full of healing. Then, simply my *presence* is releasing and helpful to the other. (p.129)

Geller and Greenberg (2002) found in their research that today presence is seen by many person-centred therapists as the deeper quality that allows for realising the core conditions.

> Presence involves being completely in the moment on a multiplicity of levels, physically, emotionally, cognitively, and spiritually. It also includes being grounded in one's self, with an expanded awareness and receptivity to others and the world around us. (Geller, 2008)

The concept of 'relational depth' is another way of promoting profound contact and healing engagement between two people. It is an attempt 'to bring the soul of our work to a higher level of awareness' (Cooper, 2006, p. 228). It is not a matter of conscious intention or willpower. I cannot make presence happen. But I can make the choice to be more or less prepared for it, more or less open, more or less centred for it to happen (Schudel, 2006). In a concrete way this has implications for me as a counsellor, so that at the beginning of an encounter I consciously make time to step back from the rush and sharpen my awareness. I sometimes sing some mantra to let go of my controlling mind and bring my consciousness to another level. I also make connection with a higher source of wisdom, a symbol of Absolute Presence, which is for me the divine Mother Mary, or which can be any form of the divine that appeals to you. There are many ways to relate to this Absolute Presence.

> Many people brought up in a Christian culture see pictures and symbols from the Christian tradition when they meditate. ... The Jesuit and Zen master Father Enomiya Lassalle gave me the following to think about: many Christians consider Buddhists to be immature because they have not yet arrived at a personal God; many Buddhists would say the same of Christians because they still stick to a personal God. 'What is it really about here?' asked Lassalle. It dawned on me that he meant presence. Absolute presence. With or without names, personal, transpersonal, beyond the transpersonal. All this is not the point. Absolute presence is undivided, not fragmented. (Schillings, 2008)

In the language of the Jungians, this is about an archetype. The archetype is the capacity to form an image, not the image itself; it is a potential with contents that are not given until they are filled in with lived experience (Corbett and Stein, 2005). For example, if the Great Mother archetype or the feminine aspect of the divine is particularly prominent in the psyche of an individual, he or she will not be attracted to a masculine God-image. The mother archetype is a transpersonal principle found in all mythologies and religious traditions. She is given local names and colouring, but, regardless of her name, there is always and everywhere a Great Mother or a Goddess who represents the feminine aspect of the divine; like Mary, Sophia, Shechina, Kali, Durga, Quan Yin, Tara, and so on. From an archetypical viewpoint, these differences in name and form are simply a matter of local folklore and emphasis. They are all manifestations of the same underlying archetypical principle.

Experience has taught me that making connection with this self-transcending source helps me to be present to extreme forms of suffering for which clients sometimes seek help. It supports me in surrendering to the process of life. It also helps me to open my heart for people or things with whom I might not usually want to make a connection.

In the therapeutic encounter sometimes I experience a qualitative jump; I can note that my style shifts to more profound developmental nurturance, fresher compassionate witnessing, more risk-taking authenticity, using opportunities of synchronicity, rather than clever engineering or complicated technical solutions. Brian Thorne (1991) captures his understanding of those moments in the following: 'I have no hesitation in saying that my client and I are caught up in a stream of love. Within this stream there comes an effortless or intuitive understanding and what is astonishing is how complex this understanding can be' (p. 77). Working from a level of soul-to-soul contact serves my development as well as that of the client. The older I grow the more I trust 'presence' as the core condition for change and growth, and I experience 'love' as the most powerful healer of the suffering soul.

The soul as a bodily felt process

The body's knowing has a unique role in the ongoing human journey into spirit. For me personally, it was a turning-point in my life when I discovered during a workshop with Gendlin what happened when the focus of attention changed to the inwardly felt body.

I was formed in an academic environment where the rational approach was self-evident. Listening to the body introduced a new development in my consciousness. The intriguing functioning of the body has had a hold on me since then. I have learned to trust it more and more.

There are different ways of paying attention to the body (Leijssen, 2006). Working with the body immediately invokes the actual. It makes one alert to what is palpable, alive and relevant. It increases self-awareness, it helps slow down responses and delays automatic behaviour. Strong affective memory can be triggered; it can resolve blocks and facilitate cathartic release. It has a stress-reducing, grounding and centring effect and, finally, it touches the transcendent ground of our lives as it is a vital doorway to the realm of cosmic consciousness.

The conceptualisation of human beings in terms of the organic principle runs through much psychotherapeutic thought (Purton, 2007). But it is equally clear that the organic pattern leaves out just what is most characteristic of human beings. As human beings we do not simply act on our strongest desires or fears, or take the homeostatic resultant of all the forces which are acting on us. For human beings desires and fears are not simple 'givens': they are open to assessment and evaluation. Some of them we wish to cultivate; others we wish to weed out. Nietzsche says that the human soul is like a garden.

> To create a garden the gardener has to take into consideration the natural propensities of various plants, the climatic conditions and so on. Creating a garden cannot be a forced, mechanical business. The organic aspect is crucial. But the gardener does not just let things grow as they will – that would produce something, but it would not create a garden. Creation requires familiarity with the natural forms and forces at play in a situation, but also a vision that will transform the situation. What makes the garden different from a merely organic system is the vision of the gardener. If we apply this to human life we see that people have the capacity to transform their desires and aversions in the light of what they experience as good or valuable. (Purton, 2002)

So a human being can make the choice to direct his or her awareness toward the bodily felt consciousness. Western science begins to discover the importance of body awareness. What is for instance called now 'mindfulness' is the western form of an ancient wisdom of the East. The capacity to be aware of what is going on in the body, has become an evidence based element of therapeutic change.

Gendlin (1996) named this bodily awareness process 'focusing'. Focusing is the process by which we become aware of the subtle level of knowing which speaks to us through the body. The word 'body' is used here, not to indicate the 'complex machine' we can look at from the outside, but the *inwardly felt body,* the living process that grows by itself in interaction with its environment. The body that knows about what we value, about what has hurt us and how to heal it. The body that knows the right next step to bring us to a more fulfilling and rewarding life. The human being, the body, is understood as a process that is environmental from the very beginning; in fact the body cannot exist without its environment. We live our situations with our bodies and the body knows how life should be lived.

Gendlin (1984) also gave the new name 'felt sense' to the experience of body sensations which are *meaningful*. The felt sense is a holistic physical sense of a situation. It transcends what is known on the levels of behaviour, emotion and cognition, and brings meaning from a new level when all these function implicitly in one whole bodily sense. As the person spends time with the felt sense, new and clearer meanings emerge. The bodily felt sense can open into a whole field of intricate details and, of its own accord, it brings the exact word, image, memory, understanding, new idea, or action step which is needed. The physical body, in response, will experience some easing or release of tension as it registers the 'rightness' of what comes from the felt sense. Therapeutic change is bodily and feels good, even if the content we are dealing with is painful. This easing of tension is what tells us that we have made contact with this deeper level of awareness and that we are on the right path (www.focusing.org Focusing-Oriented Psychotherapy).

There are strong resemblances between descriptions of the *soul* and Gendlin's concept of the *felt sense*. Gendlin introduced the new word 'felt sense' to prevent other contents that people carry with regard to religion coming to mind when one hears the word 'soul'. When one uses the publicly known language, one cannot possibly by such a word express something that is in a process of forming (Lou, 2008). And the word 'soul' is a word which has collected all kinds of concepts and meanings through the centuries that block it from being understood freshly.

For myself, at least I can say that the focusing process led to me experiencing my soul in a very concrete and vital way. My feeling that 'soul' and 'felt sense' are similar processes was confirmed by many colleagues who say that 'the soul is only shorthand for experience' (Schillings, 2008). Focusing seems to bring one closer to a point of spiritual alchemy, whereby body transmutes into soul and soul into body. So the human body plays a remarkable role in developing an awareness of spirit. What is felt in the human organism increasingly leads to a broadening of the experiential field and a finding of meaning. When we own what is really felt, our body connects to a Larger Body and shifts into a new space. Out of that connection we receive new information which in different spiritual practices is called 'revelation' and new energy which in different traditions is referred to as 'grace' (Campbell and McMahon, 1985). By carefully attending to certain experiences you could be led toward that gifted inner stream where the sense of being bodily alive in some Larger Process can unfold.

This experience originates in the body but reaches beyond the body's limits: the person feels him- or herself to be part of a Larger Process. In the words of Gendlin (1984):

> The felt sense that I also call *the edge of awareness* is the centre of the personality. It comes between the conscious person and the deep universal reaches of human nature where we are no longer ourselves. It is open to what comes from those universals, but it feels like 'really me'. (p. 81)

The felt sensing body, the soul, is connected to the whole universe. It opens up a process which implies more than we can describe in words and which incites us to reach for metaphors, symbols or images to express that 'more'. The chosen metaphors are never independent of what appeals to us in our environment.

The bodily felt experience serves as an entrance gate, and the attitude of a friendly, non-judging presence at what is experienced here and now is cultivated as crucial. When we teach focusing, finding a positive relationship to the experiencing process can be a big stumbling block for the patient. Indeed, the effectiveness of the process depends a great deal on the quality of the interaction. That is why for most people the presence of a companion is crucial for finding a caring welcoming attitude to their bodily felt experiencing process. Or, even more; the process gains considerably more depth in the presence of a good listener. By bringing an accepting and interested presence in the relationship with the client, the counsellor helps the client to listen for the freshly emerging meanings in his or her process. Clients can dig much more deeply into distressing aspects of their background, because they feel secure in the presence of a listener that would treat their experience in a non-judgmental way. So by providing this specific kind of relationship and by inviting the patient to pay attention to the inwardly felt experiencing process, the counsellor opens the way for the patient to realize the full potential of the soul.

The ultimate healing process

Finally I want to say that – although I rely on evidence-based counselling – my understanding of change and healing is different from the classical understanding of the nature of change. In my approach, the emphasis isn't just on the counsellor's responsiveness. Rather the counsellor's responses are for the purpose of helping the client be present to his/her own experience and finding the way to his or her soul (Leijssen, 2007). It is about cultivating an inner loving relationship; the ability of the client to be present to his or her own emergent experience in a welcoming, nonjudgmental way. This is an important part of the development of the client's capacity to put aside known patterns, and listen with open interest to what is emerging inside. This capacity is also necessary for sustaining attentiveness to the Mystery and listening to the movement of the Spirit or the Divine. As a counsellor I am listening to the person's unfolding process and I am also open to that higher dimension, whatever its name is that speaks to us. Through the process of pivoting between the attentiveness to the client and the mystery of the High Spirit, I invite the client to listen how the High Spirit is contributing to this process of healing. I want to sustain openness to the ineffable, immeasurable, yet real activity of the Divine that works beyond our wills, our techniques and our understanding. The ultimate healing process involves a connection between and beyond the counsellor/client relationship, including the possibility of a Divine Intervention.

References

Buber, M (1970) *I and Thou*. New York: Scribner.

Campbell PA & McMahon, EM (1985). *Bio-Spirituality: Focusing as a way to grow*. Chicago: Loyola University Press.

Cooper, M (2006) Editorial: Meeting at relational depth. *Person-Centered & Experiential Psychotherapies, 5*(4), 227–8.

Corbett, L & Stein, M (2005) Contemporary Jungian approaches to spiritually oriented psychotherapy. In: L Sperry & EP Shafranske (eds) *Spiritually Oriented Psychotherapy* (pp. 51–74). Washington, DC: American Psychological Association.

Deurzen, E van (1997) *Everyday Mysteries: Existential dimensions of psychotherapy*. London: Routledge.

Elkins, DN (2005) A humanistic approach to spiritually oriented psychotherapy. In: L Sperry & EP Shafranske (eds) *Spiritually Oriented Psychotherapy* (pp.131–52). Washington, DC: American Psychological Association.

Geller, S & Greenberg, LS (2002) Therapeutic presence: Therapists' experience of presence in the psychotherapeutic encounter. *Person-Centered & Experiential Psychotherapies, 1*(1&2), 144–55.

Geller, S (2008) Therapeutic presence. Second Life!? Congres VVCEP-VCgP, abstract from lecture, 7/11/2008.

Gendlin, ET (1984) The client's client: The edge of awareness. In: RF Levant & JM Shlien (eds) *Client-Centered Therapy and the Person-Centered Approach: New directions in theory, research and practice* (pp. 76–107). New York: Praeger.

Gendlin, ET (1996) *Focusing-Oriented Psychotherapy*. New York: Guilford Press.

Griffith, JL & Griffith, ME (2002) *Encountering the Sacred in Psychotherapy*. New York: Guilford Press.

Leijssen, M (2006) The validation of the body in psychotherapy. *Journal of Humanistic Psychology, 46*(2), 126–46.

Leijssen, M (2007) *Tijd voor de ziel*. Tielt: Lannoo.

Leijssen, M (2008) Encountering the sacred: Person-centered therapy as a spiritual practice. *Person-Centered & Experiential Psychotherapies, 7*(3), 218–25.

Lou, N (2008) Thinking at the edge. www.nadalou.com. Accessed on 30th May 2008.

Pargament, KI (2007) *Spiritually Integrated Psychotherapy. Understanding and addressing the sacred*. New York, London: Guilford Press.

Purton, C (2002) Focusing on focusing: The practice and the philosophy. www.focusing.org/fot/ Accessed on 20th May 2008.

Purton, C (2007) *The Focusing-Oriented Counselling Primer*. Ross-on Wye: PCCS Books.

Rogers, CR (1961) *On Becoming a Person. A therapist's view of psychotherapy*. Boston: Houghton Mifflin.

Rogers, CR (1980) *A Way of being*. Boston: Houghton Mifflin.

Rogers, CR (1989) A newer psychotherapy 1942. In: H Kirschenbaum & VL Henderson (eds) *The Carl Rogers Reader* (pp. 63–76). Boston: Houghton Mifflin.

Schillings, A (2008) Stillness and awareness from person to person.

www.focusing.org/spirituality/stillness.htm. Accessed on 25th May 2008.

Schudel, DI (2006) A person-centred therapist's quest for presence. In: J Moore & C Purton (eds) *Spirituality and Counselling: Experiential and theoretical perspectives* (pp. 127–35). Ross-on-Wye: PCCS Books.

Snyder, C & Lopez, S (2001) *Handbook of Positive Psychology.* Oxford: University Press

Sperry, L & Shafranske, EP (eds) (2005) *Spiritually Oriented Psychotherapy.* Washington, DC: American Psychological Association.

Thorne, B (1991) *Behold the Man.* London: Darton, Longman & Todd.

Thorne, B (2006) The gift and cost of being fully present. In: J Moore & C Purton (eds) *Spirituality and Counselling. Experiential and theoretical perspectives* (pp. 35–47). Ross-on-Wye: PCCS Books.

3

What We Are Meant to Be: Evolution as the transformation of consciousness

Jeff Leonardi

The world is a-building. (Teilhard de Chardin, 1965, p. 92)

My main thesis is this: there appears to be a formative tendency at work in the universe. (Rogers, 1980, p. 124)

We know that the whole creation has been groaning as in the pains of childbirth until now. (St Paul, Romans, 8:22)

One of the apparent collision points between secular and religious understanding can be found in their different accounts of human origins and development. Stated simplistically, science posits a causeless Big Bang at creation, and an entirely random process of inorganic and organic evolution thereafter. Christianity asserts an uncaused Creator and divine design.

These two can be taken as incompatible world views, or they can be seen to overlap. I, like most scientists *and* Christians I know, cannot rationally comprehend how something can come from nothing (causeless Big Bang) or how God could have existed un-caused from eternity. My personal response to these questions is to invoke the concept of mystery and not-knowing (in Christianity the *apophatic* approach), and I find the causeless Big Bang as intriguingly mystical as the concept of a Deity. Once initial creation has occurred I find no fundamental incompatibility between faith in God and an evolutionary understanding of matter and life.

My particular focus in this chapter is to ask questions, not about how we got here, but about where we are going, and want to

This chapter is a development of a presentation under the same title to the Keele University Counselling Conference 'Counselling and Transformation', 26th – 28th March 2010.

go? Many are fearful about the future of the human race and our world, and with good reason, e.g., James Lovelock:

> The main problem is that we're not really clever enough as a species. We haven't developed far enough. The Earth's evolving and we're evolving with it – but it's a damn slow process. It's taken us a million years to change from being semi-intelligent animals to what we are now: still animals, and still semi-intelligent. I don't think we can handle big problems like the Earth. (Lovelock, 2010)

If we are to survive and develop further, then we are going to need greater aptitudes of wisdom and cooperation between individuals and groups, including nations. Evolution as we understand it seems to be directional, i.e. towards greater complexity and successful adaptation to the environment. Human evolution includes significant development of artistic and creative endeavour, far beyond the strictly functional.

If we accept that we are the product of millennia of evolutionary development, then it seems to me to be appropriate and important to speculate about the future direction and nature of our further evolution, not just about what might happen, but about how we might wish to develop, how we might conceive the direction this might take, and how we might choose to consciously cooperate with such a continuing process.

Much of our recent human development has involved external scientific and technological 'mastery' of our world and its inhabitants, and this has brought great benefits in terms of material well-being for many. There has also been a downside in terms of unequal distribution of wealth and power, despoliation of the earth's resources and pollution of the environment, and a greater and quite terrifying increase in our capacity for destructiveness by weaponry. We are also clearly at the point where our capability for changing our genetic inheritance by technological means is likely to accelerate and questions about the wisdom of doing so are likely to be asked retrospectively i.e. if something can be done it is likely to be done before the wisdom of doing so is established. Many of the questions about 'acting like gods' are rejected by the secular media and scientific establishment as the anachronistic utterances of discredited systems of belief.

In this way, faith and trust in science and technology have had a considerable impact on the erstwhile dominance of religious world-views, and could be said to have supplanted them, to some extent. My sense is that these trends now need a counterbalancing attention to inner personal worlds, to the pursuit of wisdom, communication, relationship and understanding, and spirituality. If we have developed the means to destroy ourselves and our world, then we clearly need to develop the corresponding wisdom and means not to do so.

In this paper I should like to 'dream dreams' of what our future evolution might entail, with the help of three sources: Carl Rogers, Teilhard de Chardin and the mystical theology and anthropology of the Eastern Orthodox Christian tradition. Carl Rogers clearly understood that his work partook of an evolutionary perspective, and spoke of the 'persons of tomorrow' as we shall see; Teilhard de Chardin was both a scientist and a Jesuit Christian priest, and in his work he combined both perspectives powerfully, as we shall also see. His work was banned from publication by the Vatican until after his death. Carl quoted him as one of his heroes, and Carl also believed that the positivistic academic culture of the 20th century would not accept his (Carl's) theories, but that a later time would. The Orthodox tradition is a vast area to address, but here we will focus particularly upon its embracing of the God-givenness of human nature and potential.

The person of tomorrow

An evolutionary perspective undergirds a great deal of the Person-centred approach. The concepts of the *formative* and *actualising* tendencies are both predicated upon a sense of the universe and its components, organisms and individuals, growing, and growing towards further stages of development. Beyond, and including, human life, Rogers posits a universal *formative tendency*, a directional tendency towards increased order and interrelated complexity in all that exists:

> My main thesis is this: there appears to be a formative tendency at work in the universe, which can be observed at every level.... we

need to recognize fully... the ever operating trend toward increased order and interrelated complexity, evident at both the inorganic and the organic level. (Rogers, 1980, pp. 124–6)

Rogers is here arguing that *syntropy* is the counterbalancing tendency to entropy at every level, and links it to *the actualising tendency*: 'The inherent tendency of the organism to develop all its capacities in ways which serve to maintain or enhance the organism' (Rogers 1959, p 196). Thus the actualising tendency is 'the organismic embodiment of the formative tendency' (Bohart, 2007, p. 49). The actualising tendency in human beings is expressed, or experienced as, the *organismic valuing process,* and amounts to creativity:

...the directional trend which is evident in all organic and human life – the urge to expand, extend, develop, mature – the tendency to express and activate all the capacities of the organism, or the self.... It is this tendency, which is the primary motivation for creativity as the organism forms new relationships to the environment in its endeavour, most fully to be itself. (Rogers, 1961, p. 351)

In *A Way of Being*, Rogers subscribes to an evolutionary view which incorporates the spiritual:

And perhaps we are touching the cutting edge of our ability to transcend ourselves, to create new and more spiritual directions in human evolution. (Rogers, 1980, p. 134)

In the concluding chapter he attempts to depict the future, both in terms of trends, and in terms of 'the Person of Tomorrow'. The latter section integrates the desirable outcomes of the Person-centred approach with Rogers' sense of how people at their best were behaving and developing in various areas of social life, especially those to do with education and community development, therapy and consciousness-raising, ecology and social action. He suggests that for a viable and sustainable world of the future, the person of the future will embody some or all of the twelve qualities or traits that he names, and claims to perceive already in such people in his present experience. These qualities were:

1. Openness.
2. Desire for authenticity.
3. Scepticism regarding science and technology.
4. Desire for wholeness.
5. The wish for intimacy.
6. Process persons.
7. Caring.
8. Attitude toward nature.
9. Anti-institutional.
10. The authority within.
11. The unimportance of material things.
12. A yearning for the spiritual.
    (Rogers, 1980, *A Way of Being,* pp. 350–2)

Rogers develops each of these descriptions at some length, but for our purposes it is perhaps particularly his inclusion of 12: 'A yearning for the spiritual', which most deserves further elucidation:

> These persons of tomorrow are seekers. They wish to find a meaning and purpose in life that is greater than the individual. Some are led into cults, but more are examining all the ways by which humankind has found values and forces that extend beyond the individual. They wish to live a life of inner peace. Their heroes are spiritual persons – Mahatma Gandhi, Martin Luther King, Teilhard de Chardin. Sometimes, in altered states of consciousness, they experience the unity and harmony of the universe. (Rogers, ibid., p. 352)

There are comparisons here with the later stages of James Fowler's theory of faith development (Fowler, 1981; Wolski Conn, 1986). At Stage 5 of this theory, 'Inclusive Faith' there is recognition of our interdependence as human beings, a wider understanding of community (than the narrow and selfish), a desire to care for all people, and responsiveness to 'the transcendent call of duty' manifested in self giving service to others (Wolski Conn, p. 231).

Stage 6 is said to be characterised by the relinquishing and transcending of the self as the ultimate reference point. Persons who are deemed to be at this stage are said to have 'found' themselves by 'losing' themselves in service to others. Suggested examples of persons at this stage include Mother Teresa, Dag Hammerskjold, Martin Luther King, and Gandhi. Fowler suggests that they are characterised by a view of life as a unity which transcends paradoxes and unites seeming opposites; and by love for all people. Such people commit themselves to working to transform the world for good, often at real cost to themselves, being vulnerable to the power of those whose values they challenge, yet whose person they continue to value, and are willing to spend and be spent, often dying in the process (Wolski Conn, 1986, p. 232).

In another paper (Leonardi, 2006) I argue that there a significant comparison can be made between the Person-centred concept of the actualising tendency in human beings, and the Christian (and more general) concept of self-giving, and this is developed at greater length in my PhD thesis (Leonardi, 2008), especially in Chapter 2: *The Spirituality of the Person-centred Approach*, and Chapter 4: *Comparisons between Person-centred and Christian Spiritualities.* In the light of what has been written here and in those documents I am inclined to suggest that self-giving love is the defining characteristic of the fully functioning person in both Person-centred and religious terms.

Teilhard de Chardin

Our second source is Pierre Teilhard de Chardin, whose scientific training and orientation combined with his Christian faith to produce a mystical and evolutionary theology. His vision is capable of being articulated in orthodox Christian terms, whilst being also radical and challenging, and the response of the institutional church to him was cautious and even critical.

Through the study of fossils he became convinced of the evolutionary principle at work in the world, and found no difficulty in discerning there God's continuing engagement with creation. Viewing the human being as part of the divine evolutionary plan, he believed that Christ exemplified the end point or culmination of this process – the 'Omega point' – but that the rest of human beings were also destined for such a destiny, i.e. to attain to Christ-likeness.

For Teilhard, Jesus Christ, the Omega point of all history, is the unique self-disclosure by God of God's nature in human form, the conclusion and consummation of all creation, not just the human, to which all time is directed, both past and future. In that sense the 'Christ event' radiates forwards and backwards in time and also in eternity.

Teilhard is a profoundly incarnational[1] Christian theologian, recognising the activity of God in all creation and quintessentially in the life, death and resurrection of Jesus. His scientific intelligence embraced evolutionary theory and therefore led him to posit the evolution of the human being as central to God's purposes and fulfilled in Christ, who is thereby the forerunner and exemplar of the species.

> Teilhard's Christianity is optimistic about human nature, and the direction and purpose of life, as well as acknowledging 'the tremendous challenge and responsibility of being human'. In common with all Christianity, he sees the human enterprise as a shared task and as developing towards a 'shared destiny of the human community'. (King, 1997, p. 33)

An evolutionary perspective is so vast that we might fear that the individual, her value and significance, might become lost:

> But for Teilhard there exists a dialectical relationship between growing personalisation and increasing socialisation, the centre ring of the human person and the strengthening of bonds between persons in the human community. (King, ibid., p. 45)

A sign and expression of this bonding between human beings at the spiritual level, Teilhard claimed, was the emergence of the *noosphere*, an ethereal 'web' or network connecting all humanity around the world: 'a sphere of human thought and love, of knowing,

---

1. The Christian doctrine of the *Incarnation* consists in the belief that God became a human being in Jesus Christ, that in this way the human being 'created in God's image and likeness' (Genesis 1.26) becomes truly the God-being, and through this 'forerunner' all human beings may attain to this human–divine union; and that beyond this all of physical Creation bears the divine imprint.

acting and bonding' (ibid.) with a compelling contribution to make to the further development of the human community.[2]

Unusually in the western tradition, Teilhard embraces divinisation as an evolutionary concept:

> To come up to his full measure, *he* (the human being) *must become conscious of his infinite capacity to carry himself still further;* he must realise the duties it involves, and he must feel its intoxicating wonder. He must abandon all the illusions of narrow individuals and extend himself, intellectually and emotionally, to the dimensions of the universe: and this even though, his mind is reeling at the prospect of his new greatness, he should think that he is already in the possession of the divine, is God himself, or is himself the artisan of Godhead. (de Chardin, in King, ibid., p. 61)

For Teilhard, divinisation is an immediate and active transformation of life and activity:

> This is what he meant when he spoke of the divinisation of our activities and the divinisation of our passivities – that all that we are, all we do and all we suffer, can be transformed into a spiritual activity, thereby deeply transforming its meaning by giving it value and purpose. (King, ibid., p. 97)

Thus we find in Teilhard a Christian mystical writer who Rogers himself found congenial, as we have seen, and for whom doctrine is less important than experience – although it can of course inform experience – and for whom a Christian view of human nature is positive and even optimistic. He also could be said to be speaking directly to our times from half a century ago, in suggesting that as secular humanism discerns a dimension of human experience which – *pace* Rogers – can only be termed spiritual, so Christian religion needs to learn from our scientific and psychological knowledge:

---

2. Whether the Internet can fulfil such a high purpose, and can otherwise be seen to correspond to the noosphere, is open to argument; clearly de Chardin conceived the noosphere, not as a technological development but as an evolution of human consciousness.

> Christianity is led to the discovery, *below God,* of earthly values, while humanism is led to the discovery, *above the world,* of the place of a God. (King, ibid., p. 97)

Theosis in the orthodox tradition

The Eastern Orthodox tradition shares all the core doctrines of all the other main Christian traditions, but the additional focus given to divinisation or theosis means that many of these doctrines – Incarnation, Resurrection, Trinity – have a somewhat different emphasis. Theosis is so central to the Eastern Orthodox Church that the saying of Athanasius, that 'God became human so that humans may become God' can be described by Markides as the 'motto' of Eastern Orthodox mysticism (Markides, 2001, p. 117).

The three terms: divinisation, deification and theosis, are all equivalent, signifying 'likeness to and union with God' (Dionysius the Areopagite, in Staniloae, 2002, p. 64), and bringing all Christian souls to this state or condition is the whole goal and purpose of the Church (Staniloae, ibid., p. 64); Alfeyev states it thus:

The aim of the Christian religion is to reach the fullness of communion with God where we become united to him..... The concept of deification is central to the Eastern Orthodox theological and mystical tradition. To confess the truth faith, to be a church member, to observe God's commandments, to pray, to participate in sacraments: all these are necessary primarily because they lead to deification, the ultimate goal of everyone's existence... God made us so that we might become partakers of the divine nature and sharers in his eternity, so that we might come to be like him through deification by Grace. (Alfeyev, 2002, pp. 190–1)

That eventual union of the creature with the Creator, i.e. divinisation, is not to be understood as assimilation of the creature into the divine, where the separate personhood of the creature no longer persists, but as union between the person and God's *energies:*

> ... that is to say, in (God's) life, power, grace and glory ... The energies are truly *God* ... as he communicates himself in outgoing love. He who participates in God's energies is therefore meeting

God himself face to face, through a direct and personal union of love, in so far as a created being is capable of this. (Ware, 1979, p. 168)

It is important to note that while those who achieve – or are granted – such moments or longer periods of union with the divine are usually termed 'saints', the entire thrust and language of the Orthodox tradition with regard to theosis is that it is not the privileged territory of specialists or the 'elect', but of all Christians – or even all human beings, such is the comprehensiveness and inclusivity of the God who loves all that God has created (John 3:16).

The human being who is beginning to attain to the divine consciousness is characterised by an inclusive and unconditional love for all people and an empathy for the whole of creation:

Saint Isaac ... wrote that a truly *Eleimon*[3] heart is a heart which is on fire, consumed by love for the whole of creation, '... for human beings, birds, and wild animals, daemons, and every creature on earth. An extreme empathy towards the whole of Creation renders such a heart incapable of hearing of any hurt or even of a minor sorrow taking place within Creation. For this reason the *Eleimon* heart offers prayers for the beasts and for the birds of prey, for animals and for demons, for serpents and for everything else within creation, including the enemies of truth.' (Markides, op cit., pp. 177–81)

These attributes bear comparison with the *unconditional acceptance* of the Person-centred practitioner, and the environmental awareness of Rogers' 'Persons of Tomorrow'.

The Person-centred approach is a paradigm for relationship and, just as we can infer principles for human relating from the divine 'template', so too we can extrapolate from the Person-centred paradigm of relationality to help us comprehend divine lovingness: if empathic and unconditionally acceptant qualities of relationship can be seen to lead to healing and the re-establishment of wholeness

---

3. Eleimon: characteristic of God as charitable, compassionate, and non-judgemental. (Markides, ibid., p. 251).

in human beings, they must in an important sense witness to the nature of the divine relationship and intention towards human beings (cf Teilhard on humanism and Christianity above). In the Orthodox tradition also the *Trinitarian* conception of the divine nature as three-persons-in-relationship (of love) is paralleled by the understanding that human identity and divinisation is inescapably and necessarily *relational*:

> Our humanness is realised through interpersonal relationship; there is no true person unless there are at least two persons in communication with each other. Created in the image of the triune God, we become genuinely human only through reciprocal love after the model of (the Trinity). (Ware, in Hastings, 2000, p. 186; cf. also Schmid, 2006)

The Person-centred therapeutic climate of empathic and genuine unconditional positive regard between two persons can be understood as such a relationship and has direct consequences for the growth of the client:

1. Away from the facades and the constant preoccupation with keeping up appearances.
2. Away from 'oughts' and an internalised sense of duty springing from externally imposed obligations.
3. Away from living up to the expectations of others.
4. Towards valuing honesty and realness in oneself and others.
5. Towards valuing the capacity to direct one's own life.
6. Towards accepting and valuing one's self and one's feelings whether they are positive or negative.
7. Towards valuing the experience of the moment and the process of growth, rather than continually striving for objectives.
8. Towards a greater respect for and the understanding of others.
9. Towards cherishing of close relationships and a longing for more intimacy.
10. Towards a valuing of all forms of experience and a willingness to risk being open to all inner and outer experiences, however uncongenial or unexpected.
    (Thorne, 1991, p. 35 quoting Frick, 1971, p. 179; cf. Rogers, 1961, p. 190)

These statements of developmental direction are not necessarily obviously commendable from all perspectives, and they present a particular challenge to those ideologies which place trust in external authorities and codes of conduct, but humanistic psychology has embraced them as the authentic direction for human psychological flourishing and wholeness, and thereby the foundation for 'persons of tomorrow'. The following section outlines how such human growing can be described.

The Quality of Presence

The early and middle stages of the evolution of the Person-centred approach were focussed on the necessary and sufficient *core conditions of a therapeutic relationship,* especially *empathy*, *genuineness* and *acceptance*. Much of the more recent development of the Person-centred Approach by Rogers in his later years, and by others (Mearns, Thorne, etc.) has centred on a further dimension of the core conditions, namely *the quality of presence*, and of meeting at *relational depth.* What has been said above, about divine and human relationship, can be understood as connecting to the latter concept, relational depth. In the quality of presence we can again glimpse something of the way in which therapeutic engagement unexpectedly enters upon the spiritual realm. Rogers writes about his experience in this way:

> When I am at my best, as a group facilitator or as a therapist … when I am closest to my inner, intuitive self, when I am somehow in touch with the unknown in me, when perhaps I am in a slightly altered state of consciousness, then, whatever I do seems to be full of healing. Then, simply my presence is releasing and helpful to the other … it seems that my inner spirit has reached out and touched the inner spirit of the other. Our relationship transcends itself and becomes a part of something larger. Profound growth and healing and energy are present. (Rogers, 1980, p. 129)

It might be worth remembering that Rogers was deeply suspicious of institutional religion in general and was therefore not readily given to employing spiritual language. It was precisely because his experience required such language that he became willing to write in such terms. Those of us who have also experienced such moments in individual therapy and therapy groups can also affirm the relevance of such terminology and the parallels with religious experience.

Brian Thorne developed the Person-centred theory of core conditions and presence by offering another term: *tenderness*. He explains the quality of tenderness like this:

> In the first place, it is a quality which irradiates the total person – it is evident in the voice, the eyes, in the hands, the thoughts, the feelings, the beliefs, the moral stance, the attitude to things animate and inanimate, seen and unseen. Secondly, it communicates through its responsive vulnerability that suffering and healing are interwoven. Thirdly, it demonstrates a preparedness and an ability to move between the worlds of the physical, the emotional, the cognitive and the mystical without strain. Fourthly, it is without shame because it is experienced as the joyful embracing of the desire to love and is therefore a law unto itself. Fifthly, it is a quality which transcends the male and female, but is nevertheless nourished by the attraction of the one for the other in the quest for wholeness. (Thorne, 1991, p. 76)

He then proceeds to explicate what he means by saying that when tenderness is present, something qualitatively different can occur. In doing so, he acknowledges that language for what he wishes to convey of his experience is difficult and elusive, that he 'can do no more than grope after the inexpressible' (ibid., p. 77). He is attempting to describe those 'fleeting moments' when 'the quality I am calling tenderness is present in my own interactions as a counsellor':

> Inwardly, I feel a sense of heightened awareness, and this can happen even if I am near exhaustion at the end of a gruelling day. I feel in touch with myself to the extent that it is not an effort to think or to know what I am feeling. It is as if energy is flowing through me and I am simply allowing it free passage. I feel a physical vibrancy, and this often has a sexual component and a stirring in the genitals. I feel powerful, and yet at the same time almost irrelevant. My client seems more accurately in focus: he or she stands out in sharp relief from the surrounding decor. When he or she speaks, the words

belong uniquely to him or her. Physical movements are a further confirmation of uniqueness. It seems as if for a space, however brief, two human beings are fully alive, because they have given themselves and each other permission to risk being fully alive. At such a moment, I have no hesitation in saying that my client and I are caught up in a stream of love. Within this stream, there comes an effortless or intuitive understanding and what is astonishing is how complex this understanding can be. It sometimes seems that I receive my client whole and thereafter possess a knowledge of him or her which does not depend on biographical data. This understanding is intensely personal and invariably it affects the self-perception of the client and can lead to marked changes in attitude and behaviour. For me as a counsellor, it is accompanied by a sense of joy which, when I have checked it out, has always been shared by the client. (ibid., p. 77)

He suggests that at such moments there may be difficulty for either or both persons in the relationship in trusting such rich and pleasurable intimacy in the face of a culture of distrust of desire. If trust can be maintained, however, then there are great rewards:

> … a number of things can happen … tears for example may flow without warning and without apparent cause or there may be a sudden release of laughter. There may be an overwhelming desire for physical contact, which can result in holding hands or in a close embrace. There may be an urgent need to talk about death or God or the soul. There may be a desire to walk around or lie down….Always there is a sense of well-being, of it being good to be alive and this in spite of the fact that problems or difficulties which confront the client remain apparently unchanged and as intractable as ever. Life is good and life is impossible, long live life.' (ibid., pp. 77–8)

He concludes that tenderness enables wholeness:

> …neither I nor they can any longer be satisfied with the fragmented existence. We no longer wish to be mere facets of ourselves, and as a result, we find the courage to cross the bridge into new areas, which had previously been hidden or feared. What is more, the

> other person is perceived not as a threat to our own wholeness, but as a beloved companion who is on the same journey. We are truly members one of another. (ibid., p. 78)

For Thorne, the most significant recognition arising out of such encounter is that of 'the liberating paradox', i.e. release from the paralysis of life's contradictions, particularly those which incapacitate individuals and deprive their lives of meaning. On the contrary,

> ...in the moments of tenderness, I have experienced both my weakness and my strength and known them to be not contradictory but complementary, not paralysing but releasing. Often, too, I have known clients, who, sensing the paradox at the very source of tenderness itself, have dared to own their love–hate and have discovered that by doing so they are able to quit the emotional prison in which they were paralysed and impotent. The world of 'both and' is infinitely wider and more invigorating than the cramped conditions prevailing in the world of 'either-or'. (ibid., p. 79)

Thorne develops his understanding of the spirituality of such experiences in terms of their representing an antidote to the legacy of shame and guilt from which so many suffer and which is so potently expressed in the biblical narrative of the Fall: the loss of trust in God and therefore in ourselves as his creatures: our bodies, sexuality and desires, our very freedom of will. Thorne's claim is that in these moments of freedom and intimacy this legacy is overcome:

> For a moment, shame gives way to wholeness and the liberating paradox, and at this moment God is trustworthy, the body is trustworthy, desires are trustworthy, sexuality is not a problem, survival is not a problem, death is not to be dreaded. For a moment, perhaps a fraction of a second, we are transformed and utterly free of shame. We are restored to full friendship with God or, in secular terms, we know that we are born to be lovers and to be loved. That which I have described as qualitatively different has happened and we are never quite the same again, however much we forget, deny or deride the experience. (ibid., p. 80)

These are high claims for the potency of a therapeutic approach allied to a spiritual discipline and Thorne is careful, as in all his work, to acknowledge his sense of the danger of grandiosity and delusion. Nevertheless, like Rogers in his statement of 'presence' above, Thorne is simply declaring his experience and the understanding he has achieved of it. He acknowledges its rareness and connection to a future stage of human development:

> It will be evident that so breath taking a quality is rare. What is more no one person can hope to embody it more than fleetingly and intermittently, for to be irradiated by it is to achieve a level of humanness which belongs to the future and not to now. (Thorne, 1991, p. 76)

Conclusion

Both Thorne and Rogers believe that their commitment to embodying the core conditions of the Person-centred approach at relational depth have led them to a view of human nature and relationality which compels an acknowledgement of a spiritual perspective and description. They also, like Teilhard de Chardin before them, believe that such experience offers a glimpse of what is yet to be in a more general way, but which seems to entail the direction of human evolution if the human race is to flourish and not decay:

> And perhaps we are touching the cutting edge of our ability to transcend ourselves, to create new and more spiritual directions in human evolution. (Rogers, 1980, p. 134)

The Orthodox doctrine of theosis suggests that human development in spiritual terms is and can only be towards union with the divine and the progressive assumption of divine attributes and attitudes, summed up by a little (human and divine) word: *love*. For those for whom being fully human is a sufficient glory, with no further need for the invocation of deity, the Christian doctrine of the *Incarnation* may provide a meeting place, in that 'the glory of God is the human being fully alive' (Irenaeus).

References

Alfayev, Bishop Hilarion (2002) *The Mystery of Faith*. London: Darton, Longman & Todd.

Bohart, AC (2007) *The Actualising Person*. In: M Cooper, M O'Hara, PF Schmid, G Wyatt (eds) *The Handbook of Person-Centred Psychotherapy and Counselling* (pp. 47–63). Basingstoke: Palgrave Macmillan.

Fowler, J (1981) *Stages of Faith: The psychology of human development and the quest for meaning*. New York: Harper & Row.

Frick, WB (1971) *Humanistic Psychology: Interviews with Maslow, Murphy and Rogers*. Columbus, OH: Charles Merrill.

Hastings, A, Mason, A & Pyper, H (2000) *The Oxford Companion to Christian Thought*. Oxford: Oxford University Press.

King, U (1997) *Christ in All Things: Exploring spirituality with Teilhard de Chardin*. London: SCM.

Leonardi, J (2006). *Self-giving and Self-actualising: Christianity and the Person-centred Approach*. In: J Moore & C Purton (eds) *Spirituality and Counselling: Experiential and theoretical perspectives* (pp. 204–17). Ross-on-Wye: PCCS Books.

Leonardi, J (2008) Partners or adversaries: A study of christian and person-centred approaches to spirituality and the implications for Christian ministry and pastoral practice. PhD thesis, University of East Anglia.

Lovelock, J (2010) The *Guardian 2*, 1/6/10, p. 21.

Markides, KC (2001) *The Mountain of Silence: A search for orthodox spirituality*. New York: Doubleday.

Rogers, CR (1959) A theory of therapy, personality and interpersonal relationships, as developed in the client-centred framework. In: S Koch (ed) *Psychology: A study of science, Volume 3, Formulations of the person and the social context* (pp. 184–256). New York: McGraw-Hill.

Rogers, CR (1961) *On Becoming a Person: A therapist's view of psycho-therapy*. Boston: Houghton Mifflin; (1974) London: Constable.

Rogers, CR (1980) *A Way of Being*. New York: Houghton Mifflin.

Schmid, PF (2006) *'In the Beginning there is Community':Implications and challenges of the belief in a triune God and a person-centred approach*. Norwich: Norwich Centre Occasional Publication.

Staniloae, D (2002) *Orthodox Spirituality*. South Canaan, PA: St Tikhon's Seminary Press.

Teilhard de Chardin, P (1965) *Hymn of the Universe*. London: Collins

Thorne, BJ (1991) *Person-Centered Counselling: Therapeutic and spiritual dimensions.* London: Whurr.

Ware, Bishop K (1979) *The Orthodox Way.* Oxford: Mowbray.

Ware, Bishop K (2000) In: A Hastings, A Mason A & H Pyper (2000) *The Oxford Companion to Christian Thought.* Oxford: Oxford University Press.

Wolski Conn, J (ed) (1986) *Women's Spirituality: Resources for Christian development.* New York: Paulist Press.

4

On Faith and Nihilism:
A considerable relationship

Dave Mearns

During my service of confirmation in All Saints Episcopal Church in Glasgow in 1962 I became an atheist. I remember that it was a very clear, personal decision. Such a service is intended to focus our attention on what we are saying and doing and that focusing process helped me to hear my whole self, not only my body, *talking back*. I felt grateful for the openness of that process and I knew that I had been considerably strengthened by it. That strengthening was to be both tested and also supported by numerous experiences to come. That is what this paper is about – the effects of a personal commitment, no matter the nature of that commitment.

My first test came six weeks after confirmation when I met the vicar in the street. He was of a 'high Church' vintage, and, unusually for Glasgow, he walked the streets in back robes and not just dog collar. As altar boys we had tended to prefer when a high Church vicar was in post, because there were more interesting things to do – contrasted with the fact that the last 'low Church' vicar had an inclination towards corporal punishment in the Sunday school. I nodded and smiled at the vicar who stopped me and asked me why I had not been at Church since confirmation. 'I've joined a golf club and it's great to go there on Saturdays and Sundays.' Now, this was not a lie. At a 'presentational' level it really was my main motivation for not going to Church. Of course there was also the deeper existential basis, but, hell, that was a bit deep for a street meeting. As I told the vicar about my golf club I thought that he would share my joy – a bit naïve perhaps, but I had always got on well with him. He did not respond in that way, but he did ask me a question that proved profound. I suspect he was being sarcastic when he asked: 'Do you put golf before God?' with a disdainful emphasis on the first 'G' word. Again, for someone who had just won a powerful existential clarity, this was a great question to treat seriously even if that was not how it was being offered because I was able to look into my heart and answer him simply and without fear. 'Yes', I said. I thought we would talk some more, but he swept his robes up, and strode quickly away. I never saw him again, but since that time I was privileged to meet many other men of religion who would influence my life, not to me through their faith, but through their profound integrity.

Being clear in my lack of religious faith allowed me to be open to much of the good work the Church was doing. When we are even a little unsure of our own position, we tend to behave defensively and we cannot allow ourselves to go on to 'the other ground' lest we become further conflicted. Alternatively, when we are sure of our own position, we can reach out to the other. I became involved in running a Church youth club, soon taking sole responsibility for the Monday evening indoor football involving 50 boys in a basement church hall. An incident comes particularly to mind as the kind of 'meeting of persons' that I so value. One Monday I was visited in the basement by the leader of the Partick Cross gang, along with his four henchmen. I knew of this 17-year-old young man only from his reputation for indiscriminate violence, though I also knew that such reputations tended to be inflated by all parties. When he entered, the usual deafening noise of boys became an equally challenging silence. He stroked back his ginger hair, looked me straight in the eye and paused before speaking. I liked that – this was an interesting man. I suppose that I was so interested that I forgot to think of the fact that this pre-fire regulations basement had only one entrance/exit and Ginger plus henchmen were between me and it. 'I have had a complaint about you from one of my boys', said Ginger. When he says 'one of my boys' he is referring to the fact that in gangland Glasgow of that era, there were layers of age-grouped gangs – there was the elder 'Partick Cross', the 'Young Cross', the 'Young Young Cross' and even the 'Tiny Cross'. Ginger went on, 'He says that you threw him out last week and beat him up'. 'That must be Ritchie', I said. 'Yes, I threw him out – he completely lost the place – but I didn't touch him'. I shared his respect by also looking him straight in the eye as I spoke. I added, 'Check with the other boys'. Ginger did that over the next ten minutes, then he came back to me. 'I want to apologise to you. The story I was told was completely wrong.' He made to leave, then paused and came back. 'I want to thank you for the great work you are doing with the boys.' I nodded, in silent appreciation of this young man's gravitas. As he left, one of his henchmen grabbed poor Ritchie.

I told this story in the published Mary Kilborn lecture (Mearns, 2006) in the University of Strathclyde at the conference to mark my retirement. I also added mention of the two subsequent occasions when I met Ginger. One was about seven years later when he turned up in one of my lectures to one-year graduate students training for secondary school teaching. We spotted and recognised each other simultaneously. Ginger winked at me, partly in recognition and partly to say, 'Let's keep the past quiet'. Ten years later I met him at a conference for head teachers. This time I winked at him. People of integrity, like Ginger, can be met anywhere, if we are open to meeting them.

During my university days I had the unusual experience of living for some years with a particularly strong group of men, the majority of whom were divinity students. The context was 'The Monastery' – a small Glasgow University residence above the Church of Scotland Chaplaincy Centre at 65 Oakfield Avenue. I mention the address because, interestingly, it is now the site of the university Student Counselling Service.

There were six divinity students and four of us 'others'. There was Andy McLennan, later to become Moderator of the Church of Scotland, and after that to do commendable work in the tough role as Scottish Inspector of Prisons. There was Gus McDonald from Skye – a student of History and later head teacher who was recognised throughout his career as a man of integrity. And there was my particular favourite, Bob Brown, who later worked his heart out in parishes in the east end of Glasgow and Aberdeen. In fact, though he never knew it and we rarely met after Monastery days, Bob's integrity was a touchstone for me through most of my working life. There was also John Carrie, who so sensitively came to my room to tell me that my parents had been in a car accident and that my mother was dead. I loved these men of religion and I still do. Their integrity has been with me throughout my life.

During this time, unlike the typical student of Maths and Physics, I began to read some of the radical theology of the 1960s, like Hamilton and Altizer (1968) and Bishop John Robinson (1963), as well as earlier works by Buber (1958) and Bonhoeffer. In regard to the last mentioned I first made the mistake of attempting to read his *Ethics* (1955) rather than the intended *Letters and Papers from Prison* (1953). Anyone who knows the former work will sympathise with this poor science student.

One of the privileges of life in the Monastery was the fact that we attracted an interesting set of visitors. For example, we had visits from the Roman Catholic Chaplain, a Jesuit called Father Hughes. Wow – his was a powerful combination of intelligence and compassion. Then there was Professor Willie Barclay, who believed that theology could be written to be accessible to everyone, as in his *A Beginner's Guide to the New Testament* (see 1992 edition). His books sold better than those of other professors of divinity, but some colleagues seemed to treat his work with disdain, purely because he wrote in everyday language. When he visited I would listen intently – I also read some of his work – this man had something important for me. Now, 40 years later, I see his importance to me in every book I have written. It is perfectly possible to write in language that can be widely understood, and much of the opposite is the author's vain attempt to prove to themselves that they are smart. Willie Barclay was a welcome visitor to us young ones, but he was also an old man – we would watch him closely to note the point in the evening when he would slip his hand into his waistcoat to turn off his hearing aid and retreat into slumber!

The same university period found me involved in the Student Christian Movement (SCM). This organisation had evolved beyond its name and was, in fact, a broad collection of Christians, agnostics (I have never understood the designation) and atheists all sharing an interest in human encounter. Indeed, we ran what, in the USA, would have been called 'Encounter Groups' every lunch time from Monday to Friday. The SCM had a designated place on the steering committee of the Scottish Christian Youth Assembly (SCYA). I became that representative immediately following David Lunan, another considerable influence of integrity in my life and also later to become Moderator. Once again, in my way of thinking, the SCYA was an example of the Church doing something worthwhile. Every year it gathered 1,000 young people together for a weekend of dialogue in the Assembly Halls in Edinburgh. I served just over two years of my three-year term on the committee, being elected to be Chair in my third year. Now, it had never been a secret that I was atheist – but it didn't seem to be important – it was only important that we shared the same goals. But then I came in touch with elements in the wider world of religion. I received a total of 13 anonymous 'poison pen' letters. I can remember some of the language and it still feels frightening. I resigned, claiming pressure of work in my finals year, and remembered that the Church contains a frighteningly broad group of people. But that was not new to me – I had also exited from ultra left-wing politics when I realised that some of my colleagues would be willing to enforce their beliefs on others through violence. Any time we unite over what we believe in we need to remember that it can also be a home for collective pathology.

In the past 40 years I have had no sustained relationships with the Church and its agencies, though recently I have enjoyed just a little contact with military chaplains. I was amused to find that military chaplains from the different denominations seem to work well together with no hint of prejudicial feelings towards each other. Those prejudicial feelings are reserved for relations between the services – basically, everyone hates the Air Force! In the residential context of a conference I found myself talking quite closely with some of the chaplains. With a couple, their crisis was one of faith set in a military context, and with some others the challenge was to translate their faith into something that would be meaningful for the men and women whom they accompanied to war. Interestingly, these challenges are pretty familiar to counsellors who take their profession seriously.

One young chaplain was particularly curious about my atheism. It seemed to be a completely new experience to him to hear his faith respected and also to have dialogue about it at its depths, with someone who did not share it in any way. 'But you *behave* like a Christian!' he blurted out at one time. We then examined what he was observing in my behaviour and I openly told him how each part was linked to my secular humanism. I stopped short of offering him a treatise on existential nihilism, but I completely blew his mind with a story of a former client who, despite the fact that he knew I was an atheist, had asked me to pray with him, and I had done that. I hope that our encounter will help him in his own aim to be able to meet a wide range of humanity at some personal depth.

Having mentioned nihilism, I suppose I had better deal with it. I rarely go into this fundamental part of my grounding because many people, especially many religious people, have considerable preconceptions about nihilism – often being somewhat naïve but judgmental of it in others and afraid of any sense of it in themselves. I will give a brief account of my own concept of existential nihilism without showing the work and the pain that have led me there. To do that would radically deflect from the thread of this paper and it probably would not be able to return.

Arguably the most accessible modern philosopher of nihilism is Carlos Castaneda, through the words of his main character, a Yaqui sorcerer, Don Juan Matus in *A Separate Reality* (Castaneda, 1971) and other books. Castaneda maintained that Don Juan was real and that he had had tutelage with him over some years. Others debate the veracity of this provenance, but they miss the point, because Castaneda's supreme irony is that it whether Don Juan was real or not really does not matter. Especially heuristic is Don Juan's concept of *The Controlled Folly.* In seeking to learn from Don Juan, Castaneda's challenge is to let go his past and the way that constrains his perception in the present. This is what Carl Rogers was about. He argued that our behaviour in the present was not *caused* by our experiences in the past, but that such past history could shape the way we *perceived* our present (Rogers, 1951, pp. 491–2). Don Juan assisted the process of 'letting-go' with liberal use of peyote, but that is probably only compulsory in California and should not detract from his observations. Essentially, in Don Juan's philosophy, it is important to get to the point of realisation that, essentially, nothing 'matters'. Nothing is more important than anything else. If we come to that point, far from being despairing, it is liberating. Essentially, everything we choose to do is meaningless in absolute terms. Everything that we do is a *folly.* But, with everything lacking meaning in absolute terms, it is open to us to choose what we will attribute our personal meaning to. This then becomes a *controlled folly* – it does not cease to be a folly simply because we choose it, but the importance we attach to it is a matter of our choice and control. It is important to remember that we have no omnipotence to change the essential nature of a folly – the opposite is to attribute omnipotence to ourself and our choices (an unfortunate tendency of human beings). We will also remember that our controlled follies are no more important than those of others in an absolute sense, but we will still work hard for them because they are our choices. This philosophy of nihilism can release considerable energy in us as we strive to advance our goals. But that energy is not one that would ride roughshod over other people and their goals, because, at a fundamental existential and philosophical level, we know that our choices are no more important than those of others. So, we can listen to the world of others and their different choices without feeling threatened about our own or without needing to threaten others about theirs. Hence, our willingness to listen to others and to prize them in their difference to us is deeply grounded in our personal philosophy.

At a superficial level of comprehension, nihilism and spiritual faith might seem polar opposites. Certainly, where the doctrine of 'mission' is a driving force in the religious person there will be a huge gulf between them and the nihilistic humanist. One of the observations that has interested me in relation to people of faith is how they can be divided according to mission. There is a fundamental political difference between a religious person whose faith is a personal one and another whose faith needs them to take their mission to heretics. The first religious does not need to change others and can value others for their difference while the second needs to judge and change others. It is no wonder that many people of faith are challenged when they try to come together in the Church.

As a nihilistic humanist it is a pleasure for me to work with a religious person from the first tradition outlined above. It is interesting how we reach the same position, from different starting points, in regard to a genuine valuing of others. I like to err on the side of being simplistic in argument because I find that position is more heuristic. So, perhaps a religious person from the first tradition is coming from a faith that 'everything matters' while my basis is that 'nothing matters' (in absolute terms). We might both value each other's difference – what is much more dangerous to civilisation is the person who believes that *some* things matter.

When I work with my dear friend Brian Thorne, we come from very different yet very similar positions. We have won considerable personal knowledge of each other over 35 years of encounter. I know the potency of his faith and that it is manifested in everything he does. He knows the strength of the commitments I have made to our common areas. He knows that my philosophy carries a 'check' in it that would monitor my own actions lest I forgot that my values were no more important than those of others. I know that he is the kind of Christian who has deeply internalised his loving and that any sense of 'mission' he has is purely in terms of the example he sets as a person. We can deeply trust each other's passion. Probably there is no sounder basis for a working relationship than shared passion. When we work together as trainers we will each see differences in the ways we function. Brian is more obviously loving and more patient than I am and I find challenge a little easier. When we write together there is pride but not defensiveness in our own productions and it is easy to challenge each other. I know that a striving for communication is central to him and I admire his ability to write in a flowing style that weaves together ideas and feelings. For his part, he likes the way I can bring clients to life in our pages. We have never had a writing problem that we have not been able to solve, though, on one occasion, we deliberately took on a challenge where we knew from the outset that we would have to write separately. It was Chapter 3, entitled *The 'heart' of person-centred therapy: Spiritual and existential?* in *Person-Centred Therapy Today: New frontiers in theory and practice* (Mearns and Thorne, 2000). Early in the chapter we set out our intention:

> In this chapter each of us, in his own language, is going to speak about what we consider to be the 'heart' of person-centred therapy. Our languages are very different and we want to preserve that difference in the hope that all readers might find resonance in one or the other, if not in both. (p. 55)

In my writing within that chapter I lay out the distinctly *existential* emphasis of my working. I know that others might easily use the term *spirituality* to describe the experience of meeting a client at relational depth, but I never use that word. Though the meaning of the word 'spirituality' has broadened considerably in recent times, still, to me, it invokes the presence of the Holy Spirit. I choose not to use the concept, not because it is irrelevant to an atheist, but out of respect for those for whom it has a very special meaning. For me I find that I do not need the hypothesis of anything beyond the person because the humanity of the individual, no matter who they are, is wondrous enough and can describe the powerful experiences people have in relationship. In the chapter I set the scene for some case illustrations of the power of humanity in work with a hard-to-reach client, with an interesting aside to nihilism and divinity which went unexplained in the chapter but is relevant here:

> Yet, the reality for the person-centred therapist is that when we properly enter the existential Self of another we find ourselves simply admiring the tenacity and the beauty of the human's survival. At this point we have stopped being a representative of even the subtle 'social control' forces within our society. We have entered the territory where nihilism and divinity meet. It is time to meet Bobby, an erstwhile Glasgow gangster. (p. 57)

In my books over the last ten years, I wanted to challenge the reader with a series of clients they might be not easily feel open towards. Whether it is accurate or not, I had a suspicion that many people were confusing person-centred therapy with cotton wool. While writers like Peter F. Schmid and I would tease out the nature of relational 'encounter' in person-centred therapy (Schmid and Mearns, 2006; Mearns and Schmid, 2006), much of the quality of that relationality seemed to become diluted by the time it reached clients. Instead of the person-centred therapist being a congruent and full figure with whom the client could knock up against in order to feel their own firmness, the way many person-centred counsellors described their practice sounded as though their clients were being offered a relationship with cotton wool – soft, warm, and in that sense comforting, but of no significant relational substance. When this was combined, as it generally was, with a disinclination to 'show their working' (Mearns and Thorne, 2007, pp. 123–4) in relation to the client, supervisee or trainee, the practitioner had succeeded in taking themselves out of the work in the same way as the classical analyst, with some of the same consequences in terms of the client's entrapment in a 'game' of therapy, rather than in the reality of a therapeutic encounter. Such 'cotton wool' therapists have found a safe place to go to in order to avoid encounter, but the incongruence they have built into their working puts them in danger of burn-out in the longer term.

In my outlining of the power of *relational depth* (Mearns and Cooper, 2005), I hoped to bring the relational encounter back into attention. It has probably done that for many people, but I still find some who even see relational depth in terms of just a thicker roll of cotton wool.

The following account by a client gives a sense of what it can feel like to be offered a person rather than cotton wool.

Box 3.6 'I stopped needing to pretend'

I stopped needing to pretend. I had been in counselling three times before. They had all been good experiences and I thought that I had got a lot out of them. But this time was completely different. At first I didn't know how to take Mary [the counsellor]. She was more 'direct' than I was used to. My first thought was that she was a bit 'hard' on me. I was used to something softer. But, she could really 'meet' me more fully than anyone before. She could even meet me through my defences. Once she challenged me by asking if I was presenting what I was talking about in a particular way to her – in a way that would make her think well of me. It was an awful thing to say – but she said it really well – I felt it was coming from her understanding of me, not any 'judging' of me. I just answered, 'Yes', and looked her straight in the eye. I didn't even make my usual excuses. From that moment everything was different. I realised that I had two answers to every question – the 'pretend' one and the 'real' one. I began to give both of them. I was speaking to her in a way that was different to anything before. Even my tone of voice was different – it was less squeaky, more serious and, altogether, more 'fullsome'. I began to experience everything more fully. When I felt emotions, they were more powerful – again, more fullsome. I realised, with some horror, that I had almost never been 'real' in my life before. I had habitually 'put on a face' to the world.

With me not defending, we got to areas I had never been to before. I saw different feelings within me as well as the ones I was used to feeling. In relation to my mother's death I not only saw my sadness, but I felt my hate, and also my sorrow for her. An interesting thing was that my 'not defending' actually made me less scared. This is difficult to explain, but it is important. It wasn't just that she made it safe for me so that I didn't need to defend. It was that she challenged me as a truly caring human being and I responded. It was me responding and continuing to respond that made me less scared – there was no dependence on her. It's unusual. (Mearns and Thorne, 2007, p. 65)

As well as relational depth getting a lot of positive attention, I was genuinely surprised to find some colleagues who saw it as the antithesis of what Rogers was about. Usually they had not worked directly with Rogers but had been trained by someone who knew someone who knew Rogers during his time in Chicago. In fact, as I have often said, there is nothing new in relational depth other than Rogers' core conditions in powerful combination, except that it demands that the therapist does not settle for a dilution of those conditions.

As I mentioned earlier, in major case illustrations I began to introduce the reader to clients quite different from 'Joan' in *Person-Centred Counselling in Action* (Mearns and Thorne, 2007). Most particularly, I introduced readers to 'Bobby' (Mearns and Thorne, 2000), a former gangster who retained many of his associated skills, 'Dominic' (Mearns and Cooper, 2005), a 'hopeless drunk' (his own description) and the mute 'Rick' (Mearns and Cooper, 2005) who had shot a mother and her four children under five. I wanted to show how it was possible to 'reach' even such apparently difficult-to-reach clients by using nothing more, but also nothing less, than our humanity. I wonder how far I succeeded in my quest? Certainly, I have had a lot of good feedback about these cases and how they are written, particularly since I am willing to 'show my working' to the client and to the reader, including my obvious mistakes. Trainees particularly like the fact that I expose my mistakes – it frees them from the paralysing tyranny of believing that they always have to get it right. It would be difficult to establish a relationship at depth with a therapist who got it right all the time or, more realistically, with a therapist who didn't get it right but tried to hide that. But the writing has had its critics. Some have not liked my refusal to convert my clients' language into more politically correct forms, and one critic from the non-directive strand of the person-centred approach said that Rogers would 'turn in his grave' at my behaviour in relation to Rick. I declined to inform her that Rogers had supervised this work.

Whether or not introducing these clients has had an impact on others, it has certainly affected me. The material is so powerfully existential that it grabs us up out of our everyday, inevitably less charged, living and reminds us that there are many people who have nowhere to take their own highly charged experiencing. While, as described above, I have no inclination towards 'mission', I do think that any profession that takes itself seriously should ask why only a small percentage of the population regards its services and the way it offers them as relevant. Historically, both Brian and I have sought to support the developing profession of counselling through holding offices in the British Association for Counselling and Psychotherapy (BACP). We have also challenged the boundaries of the profession and he, more than me, has felt the consequent reactionary forces.

There is a possibility that the profession is getting close to an ossifying institutionalisation. This is a natural phenomenon – all institutions, indeed any grouping of people, seeks to norm its functioning. That is a part of the human being's efforts to make their social environment safer and more predictable. It works best if there is, simultaneously, an opposite force of 'individualisation' where the socialisation process is challenged on the restrictions it is mounting on the individuals within it. But that, in turn, relies on people being willing to exert effective challenge. Most people 'moan' rather than challenge. I remember in my training as shop steward in the Transport and General Workers Union more than 40 years ago that we were taught never to moan. As was later well established in social psychology research, moaning is a way to trick ourself into thinking that we are challenging and cover up the fact that, in our actions, we are actually conforming.

When we look at hard-to-reach clients – clients who do not obviously fit our normal counselling contexts – we are challenged to think how counselling might broaden rather than narrow what it offers and the ways it extends its offers. We are so stuck with the therapeutic hour, the comfortable office and all the other elements by which our offerings are structured. Certainly they make life comfortable for us and 10 per cent of the population, but what about the other 90 per cent? Can we take ourselves out of our immediate comfort zone to creatively meet other people who do not find our world relevant? On one of our annual training courses in Buenos Aires, I was impressed by a woman who said:

> I've got it. I realise what the real challenge of relational depth is. It's about me looking at the fact that all my counselling at present is done within my gated community. I am going to get out into the wider community instead of being scared of it.

Perhaps what our creativity will develop will be something different from counselling or perhaps we will have the effect of taking the profession with us. However we develop, the challenge to us is simply stated – to share our humanity and see the impact that may have on others. It is moving to find that both people of faith and those who have none can meet over this considerable relationship.

References

Barclay, W (1992) *A Beginner's Guide to the New Testament*. Edinburgh: Saint Andrew Press.

Bonhoeffer, D (1953) *Letters and Papers from Prison*. London: SCM Press.

Bonhoeffer, D (1955) *Ethics*. London: SCM Press.

Buber, M (1958) *I and thou* (RG Smith, Trans. 2nd ed). Edinburgh: T & T Clark.

Castaneda, C (1971) *A Separate Reality*. New York: Simon & Schuster.

Hamilton, W & Altizer, TJJ (1968) *Radical Theology and the Death of God*. Harmondsworth: Penguin.

Mearns, D (2006) The humanity of the counsellor. The 2006 Mary Kilborn Lecture. In the University of Strathclyde DVD *Meeting at Relational depth*. Ross-on-Wye: PCCS Books.

Mearns, D & Cooper, M (2005) *Working at Relational Depth in Counselling and Psychotherapy*. London: Sage.

Mearns, D & Schmid, PF (2006) Being-with and being-counter. Relational depth: the challenge of fully meeting the client, *Person-Centered and Experiential Psychotherapies, 5*, 255–65.

Mearns, D & Thorne, B (2000) *Person-Centred Therapy Today: New frontiers in theory and practice*. London: Sage.

Mearns, D & Thorne, B (2007) *Person-Centred Counselling in Action*, 3rd ed. London: Sage.

Robinson, J (1963) *Honest to God*. London: SCM Press.

Rogers, CR (1951) *Client-Centered Therapy. Its current practice, implications and theory*. Boston: Houghton Mifflin.

Schmid, PF & Mearns, D (2006) Being-with and being-counter: Person-centered psychotherapy as an in-depth co-creative process of personalization. *Person-Centered and Experiential Psychotherapies*, *5*, 174–90.

5

Mindfulness and the Person-Centred Approach

Judy Moore and Alison Shoemark

Quick now, here, now, always –
A condition of complete simplicity
(Costing not less than everything)
And all shall be well and
All manner of thing shall be well …
> (TS Eliot, 'Little Gidding', Section V, *Four Quartets;* quoted
> in Kabat-Zinn, 2005, p. 427)

Mindfulness is an ancient Buddhist practice that involves total acceptance of 'now', of the simple reality of the present moment. If practised consistently over time it leads to heightened wellbeing, a deep sense that 'all shall be well'. However, as human beings, we are easily drawn away from straightforward engagement with the present moment by memories, speculations, preferences, judgments and self-doubt. Mindfulness practice involves accepting the reality of the unfolding present, whatever it turns out to be.

The psychological benefits of this apparently simple activity have been usefully recognized over the past two decades and some of the key insights of mindfulness transmitted to the general population in the US, the UK and elsewhere in the western world through the pioneering work of microbiologist Jon Kabat-Zinn, Founding Director of the Stress Reduction Clinic at the University of Massachusetts Medical Center and cognitive psychologists Zindel Segal, Mark Williams and John Teasdale. Given the professional backgrounds of Segal, Williams and Teasdale, recent developments in terms of mindfulness as a psychological therapy have come to be associated with cognitive behavioural therapy (CBT). Yet no claims are made by its founders that this should be the case. Kabat-Zinn, a long-standing practising Buddhist at the time of his first meeting with Segal, Williams and Teasdale in 1993, describes 'sensing a deep gulf between our frames of reference' (2005, p. 439). Nevertheless, they were soon able to get beyond these differences for Segal, Williams and Teasdale to devise and establish their own mindfulness training programmes from which countless individuals have benefited over the past twenty years. The fundamental truths that enable mindfulness practice to work are those of the human condition rather than those of any specific therapeutic orientation.

Although mindfulness is at the heart of Buddhist practice, the value of being present to the 'now', of attaining 'a condition of complete simplicity' as described by T.S. Eliot in the quotation at the beginning of this chapter, has been recognized over centuries, across cultures and within different religious traditions. Kabat-Zinn, a Buddhist, quotes Eliot, an American Anglican, to illustrate what it means to arrive at the moment of 'now' and within Eliot's lines lies a further reference to the words of the medieval mystic, Julian of Norwich ('All shall be well and/all manner of thing shall be well'). This kind of multi-layered cross-referencing is typical of endeavours to communicate what is essentially beyond words: that if we can live in the present moment then, *somehow* – in a way that is beyond ordinary human comprehension – 'all shall be well'. The 'now' is both literally the present moment and the gateway to what Kabat-Zinn (2005) terms the 'orthogonal reality' in which healing occurs and where spiritual understanding may open. Eliot called it 'the intersection of the timeless moment' ('Little Gidding', Section I). In very simple terms, Ekhart Tolle (2005) has more recently described this intersection of realities as 'The Power of Now'.

The practice of mindfulness enables us to live more fully in the present and involves acceptance of what is happening in the body both physically and at the level of the felt sense as well as at the level of thoughts and emotions. Our aim in this chapter is to consider how mindfulness relates to the person as understood by the person-centred approach and how this understanding might be integrated in clinical practice. We will consider the Buddhist origins of mindfulness and give a brief account of the main developments of mindfulness as a psychological therapy, specifically as they relate to the UK, where we live and work. We will consider how mindfulness relates to the person-centred notion of 'acceptance' and how the theory and practice of focusing brings new meaning to the concept of 'acceptance', which, when brought to the level of the felt sense, can open the way to the 'orthogonal reality' of healing and ultimately of spiritual understanding.

The use of mindfulness in clinical work is exemplified through a case study recorded over five sessions at the Abertay Research Clinic in April/May 2007. Alison Shoemark reflects on her work with a client who presented with panic attacks and extreme anxiety, conditions which are regarded as particularly challenging for the person-centred approach.

Both authors have been engaged in some form of mindfulness practice since they began person-centred training in 1985. The chapter ends with a brief account of their respective journeys.

Mindfulness as a Buddhist practice

> …one continually so observes the body, *qua* body, that one remains energetic, conscious, and mindful, having disciplined both the desire and the dejection which are common in the world. Similarly, one continually so observes the sensations, thoughts, and states of mind, that one remains energetic, conscious, and mindful, having disciplined both the desire and the dejection which are common in the world; this…is what is called right mindfulness. ('Concerning the Application of Mindfulness' (*Maha Satipatthana Sutta*), Ling, 1981, p. 81)

The Buddha's teaching was focused on how we, as human beings, might find the end of suffering. Although his teachings were formulated 2,500 years ago, they are based on many years of reflection and deep understanding of the human condition. He understood and taught that 'everything changes' (*Anicca*): as a result of this we both experience loss and fear losing what we have. The First Noble Truth of Buddhism is the 'truth of suffering' (*dukkha*): we will inevitably experience change and therefore know loss and pain in our lives. The Second Noble Truth is that craving or attachment ('inner thirst' or *tanha*) leads to a further layer of unhappiness/dissatisfaction developing in us and becoming the background to our existence. If we were able simply to accept the loss and pain that comes to us, to observe the rise and fall of fears and desires instead of fuelling them and acting on them we would lessen our suffering. This leads to the Third Noble Truth, which is that we will free ourselves from chronic unhappiness or dissatisfaction only if we give up the habit of attachment and accept life as it actually is.

MacPhillamy (2003) explains that giving up the habit of craving/ attachment or, in the words of the *Satipatthana Sutta* quoted above, '[disciplining] both the desire and the dejection which are common in the world' presents a near-impossible challenge. He likens it to giving up an addiction because we generally distract ourselves from the suffering that arises from attachment by various intoxicants, such as greed, anger (sometimes described as 'hate') and delusion. 'Anger' and 'delusion' are the most interesting of these when viewed from a therapeutic perspective. 'Anger' MacPhillamy describes as 'raw emotion' (2003, p.14) which feeds upon itself, leads to actions that fuel anger in others and ultimately leads to more anger and distress. 'Delusion' he describes as the most serious of the three intoxicants because it '[keeps] people unaware of what is actually going on, both within themselves and in the world around them' (2003, p.16). Variants on 'delusion' can involve a sense that we are powerless and have no responsibility for our lives, a sense that we are inadequate, incompetent, worthless- or perhaps that we are simply too busy or preoccupied to give attention to what is really going on inside us.

The way out of this state of chronic unhappiness is the Fourth Noble Truth, the Noble Eightfold Path, which offers practical steps as to how we might become fully present in the world in a way which leads to truth, peace and ultimately the satisfaction of living from the inner 'Buddha' nature that is present in us all. The steps of the Path are Right Understanding; Right Thought; Right Speech; Right Action; Right Livelihood; Right Effort; Right Mindfulness and Right Meditation. All the steps are based on accepting the truth of things as they are. In Soto Zen, the tradition from which MacPhillamy writes, meditation involves paying close attention to the fact of simply sitting as a physical body in which thoughts and feelings arise. From a slightly different Zen perspective, Thich Nhat

Hahn writes: '... when mindfulness is present ... the seven other elements of the eightfold path are also present' (1993, p. 24).

Mindfulness, staying in conscious awareness of that which is true, within the changing processes and distractions of everyday life can thus be seen as the foundation of Buddhist philosophy and practice. It is fundamentally a *grounded* awareness of reality. It this awareness that Jon Kabat-Zinn sought to bring to patients suffering from chronic physical disorders at the University of Massachusetts Hospital in setting up the Stress Reduction Clinic there in the 1970s.

Mindfulness as a psychological therapy

The Noble Eightfold Path consists of steps designed to facilitate an inner revolution in consciousness. Jon Kabat-Zinn had originally trained as a microbiologist and sought to bring understanding from his Zen Buddhist practice to bear on patients who were suffering from intractable medical conditions that led not only to physical discomfort but also to psychological stress. In one experiment patients suffering from psoriasis were divided into two groups, one of which was given mindful meditation instructions during uncomfortable ultraviolet skin treatment and the other was not. It was found that the meditators healed at approximately four times the rate of the non-meditating control group (Kabat-Zinn et al., 1998). Kabat-Zinn's work was gradually extended to individuals suffering from depression and anxiety in different parts of the community.

At the Massachusetts Stress Reduction Clinic individuals are offered a structured programme in mindfulness, with the aim of enabling participants to bring their full attention to whatever they are experiencing in the present moment. In addition to meditation and some yoga practices, a significant feature of these programmes is the body scan, where detailed attention is brought to each area of the body in turn. The aim is not to become more relaxed, but simply to become more aware. There are interesting similarities between the body scan and working with direct bodily experiencing in Wholebody Focusing as devised by Kevin McEvenue (e.g. Van der Kooy and McEvenue, 2006).

In *Mindfulness-Based Cognitive Therapy for Depression* (2002) Zindel Segal, Mark Williams and John Teasdale give a full and very readable account of how, in seeking to help depressed patients to disengage from the kind of entrenched negative thinking that perpetuates depression, they discovered the value of mindfulness through the work of Jon Kabat-Zinn. Following their first meetings in the early 1990s, Kabat-Zinn insisted that they should themselves practise what they were proposing to teach and this has remained a fundamental principle for all those teaching Mindfulness-Based Stress Reduction (MBSR) programmes. Borrowing significantly from the MBSR programmes, Segal, Williams and Teasdale devised a programme that their own patients could follow that involves learning to meditate, learning how to be more fully aware of the body, and how to notice, with some degree of detachment, what is arising in the mind, the feelings that thoughts might trigger – and how thoughts and feelings come and go. They found that mindfulness training significantly reduces the chance of relapse for individuals who have already had three or more episodes of depression. The programme that they have devised is known as Mindfulness-Based Cognitive Therapy (MBCT) and the treatment, the basis for it and its evaluation are fully outlined in the book. Of particular interest is their observation that a particular kind of ruminative thinking is likely to play a part in the generation and maintenance of recurrent depression and that one of the key achievements of mindfulness programmes is to bring about a 'switch' of mode from 'doing' to 'being':

> The core skill that the MBCT program aims to teach is the ability, at times of potential relapse, to recognize and disengage from mind states characterized by self-perpetuating patterns of ruminative, negative thought…. In order to do this, participants have to learn how to disengage from one mode of mind and enter another, incompatible, mode of mind…. This involves moving from a focus on content to a *focus on process*, away from cognitive therapy's emphasis on changing the content of negative thinking, toward *attending to the way all experience is processed*. (2002, p. 75; our emphasis)

Over the past two decades mindfulness programmes, both MBSR and MBCT, have proliferated in the UK, though such trainings as those run by the Centre for Mindfulness Research and Practice at the University of Bangor, the work of the Centre for Suicide Research at the University of Oxford (where Mark Williams is now based) as well as through a variety of mindfulness programmes run independently through Buddhist centres throughout the country. In Scotland mindfulness is widely used in medical settings as a form of psychological therapy. The concept of mindfulness has been developed to include education, with courses run for teachers and an intention to run courses for senior school pupils. In response to the growing interest in applying mindfulness to every day life settings, Aberdeen University is currently running a secular mindfulness programme in partnership with Samye Ling Buddhist Centre in Scotland. Holy Isle (Lamlash), a small island off the south of the isle of Arran and owned by the Rokpa Trust, offer and host many courses focusing on mindful practice.

Many person-centred practitioners, ourselves included, have had experience of mindfulness training programmes and over the past decade attempts have been made to integrate some of the insights from mindfulness into clinical work. David Elias, who currently teaches at Bangor, wrote an MA dissertation on the compatibility of the person-centred approach and the Buddhist concept of mindfulness (2001). Kathleen Madigan, who has trained both in mindfulness at Bangor and in the person-centred approach at the University of East Anglia, writes in her own MA dissertation that she sees mindfulness-based approaches as the 'natural companion of the person-centred approach' (2006:2). Shari Geller in a PCEP Journal article (2003) meanwhile considers Experiential Psychotherapy in relation to mindfulness meditation:

> Mindfulness involves a development of awareness and an open and willing acceptance of all internal states that arise during meditation.... Meditation provides an opportunity to allow the confusion to be there, rather than sorting out the confusion as therapy does. (2003, p. 261)

More recently, Manu Bazzano (2010) has written of his research into the impact of meditation practice on the work of person-centred practitioners.

We would like to take these considerations a little further by looking at some of the overlap between Kabat-Zinn, Segal, Williams and Teasdale's work and concepts that are central to the person-centred approach.

Some implications for the person-centred approach

[Mindfulness] practice aims to explore the consequences of reversing the habitual tendency of the mind to move *away* from the painful/ difficult. This is done through intentionally bringing awareness (a gentle, kindly, friendly awareness) *to* the sense of how the difficult is manifesting *in the body*, including aversion-related physical sensations. In this way, one can begin to reverse one's habitual rejection of the difficult and the unpleasant, and cultivate an attitude of acceptance and friendliness. Bringing a gentle curiosity to something is, itself, part of acceptance. Holding something in awareness is an implicit affirmation that we can face it, name it, and work with it. (Segal, Williams and Teasdale, 2002, p. 228; original emphasis.)

The body and the processing of experience

Mindfulness involves bringing awareness first and foremost to the body. The *Maha Satipatthana Sutta* describes mindfulness as the act of bringing awareness to the 'body' and 'to sensations, thoughts, and states of mind' and, in the opening quotation of this section, Segal, Williams and Teasdale stress that awareness needs to be brought '*to* the sense of how the difficult is manifesting *in the body*'. Moreover, Segal, Williams and Teasdale also consider mindfulness to involve 'moving from a focus on content to a focus on process… toward *attending to the way all experience is processed*' (2002, p.75; quoted above). These statements bring us directly to the insights that the person-centred approach gains from the work of Eugene Gendlin. Gendlin makes a distinction between 'experience', which relates to the content of our lives and 'experiencing', the processing of that content, which, Gendlin stresses, takes place in the body: 'It is something present, directly referred to and *felt*' (1997a, p. 243; original emphasis).

In our view, working mindfully in a person-centred way involves a necessary shift from 'content' to 'process', to working with the client in such a way as to enable them to listen to 'the sense of how the difficult is manifesting *in the body*'. It essentially involves accepting a 'process' view of the person, such as that elaborated by Gendlin in *A Process Model* (1997b).

Accepting a process view of ourselves in this way brings about a significant shift. In terms of cognitive therapy this is seen as a shift from an emphasis on 'changing the content of negative thinking' to 'attending to the way all experience is processed'. In terms of the person-centred approach it similarly involves a shift: from an emphasis on feeling or emotion to 'attending to the way all experience is processed'. This is explained by Campbell Purton (2004) in an image which anticipates the metaphor of 'opening the box' described in the case example below:

> Experiencing which is already packaged-up in terms of familiar emotion terms is not open to change. What the focusing-oriented therapist tries to do is to help the client re-open the package. The client's experiencing is always much richer than the emotion labels which have become attached to it, and it is only from that implicit and more intricate experiencing that change can come. (p. 133)

Acceptance, 'Orthogonal Reality' and 'Therapeutic Stoppage'

Giving attention to that which simply 'is' in terms of the ongoing process of experiencing brings new meaning to the concept of 'acceptance', again one that is explored by Purton (2004). The acceptance of mindfulness involves a non-judgmental openness, a 'gentle curiosity' towards what comes, an attitude that, Purton writes, is also present in the focusing-oriented person-centred therapist:

> The therapist can help the client by adopting towards the client just that unconditional acceptance which the client needs to adopt towards their own experiencing. (p. 200)

Purton sees this level of acceptance as that which is encompassed by Dave Mearns' notion of 'relational depth', where the acceptance is not simply of the client as a person of worth but for the depths of their existential experiencing (Mearns, 1997; Mearns and Cooper, 2005). Again, this anticipates a significant moment in the case example below where the therapist realizes that she was striving to establish a 'relationship' with the client, but that what the client needed was a deeper kind of acceptance, 'a deeply accepting, compassionate space, with no judgment and vitally, not just from me to her, but from her to herself' (see case example below).

The level of acceptance that is indicated by mindfulness has profound implications. Kabat-Zinn makes it clear that bringing acceptance and curiosity to all that one is experiencing opens the way to a potential shift in consciousness. The nature of the questions that are asked begin to change, to take on more universal significance, as the client in the case example begins to ask: '*could the mind be sore… how can it show pain?*' and '*Is it all linked?*' In this respect we can see the connection between the simple acceptance of moment-by-moment experiencing and the Buddhist path. First we have to know the truth of the self and this leads to a self-forgetting that ultimately opens the way to another, larger reality:

When one studies Buddhism one studies oneself; when one studies oneself, one forgets oneself; when one forgets oneself one is enlightened by everything and this very enlightenment breaks the bonds of clinging to both body and mind not only for oneself but for all beings as well. (Great Master Dogen, Jiyu-Kennett, 1999, p. 206; quoted in Moore, 2004, p. 118)

Kabat-Zinn (2005) explains this process as a 'rotation in consciousness' that leads to an opening up to an 'orthogonal reality':

The process feels like nothing other than an awakening from a consensus trance, a dream world, and thus all of a sudden acquiring multiple degrees of freedom, many more options for seeing and responding and for meeting wholeheartedly and with mindfulness whatever situations we find ourselves in, that before we might have just reacted to out of deeply embedded and conditioned habits. It is akin to the transition from a two-dimensional 'flatland' into a third special dimension, at right-angles (orthogonal) to the other two. Everything opens up, although the two 'old' dimensions are the same as they always were, just less confining. (p. 350)

What is described here is a truth of the human condition and the spiritual path is simply a path with many stages and occasional moments of opening to a 'third special dimension'. In the therapeutic relationship we are simply working with a snapshot of reality where the therapist's empathy and use of self are directed to greater awareness of moment-by-moment experiencing of both self and other, wherever that may lead. Significant shifts, such as that experienced by Theresa in the case example below, can occur in even very brief therapy because the client can, in a very short time, find through mindfulness a place of 'awareness' that is intrinsically healing and helpful:

That part of you that is mindful is just seeing what is transpiring from moment to moment, nothing more. It is not rejecting the bad, it is not condemning anything or anybody, it is not wishing that things were different, it is not even upset. Awareness, like a field of compassionate intelligence located within your own heart, takes it all in and serves as a source of peace within the turmoil, much as a mother would be a source of peace of peace, compassion, and perspective for a child who was upset. (Kabat-Zinn,1996, p. 324)

This process is akin to what Yasuhiro Suetake, in his recent consideration of the clinical implications of *A Process Model*, defines as 'therapeutic stoppage'. This kind of 'stoppage' involves 'stopping an idle-running process in the client, which is psychopathological in some cases'. Suetake explains that this is not merely a technical intervention:

Rather it requires a quality of presence such that therapist's whole person is engaged in making a safe space for the client to feel all right without repeating the given process.... Such *therapeutic stoppage* should be given its rightful place in therapy. (2010, p. 124; original emphasis)

Suetake is one of the main exponents of Gendlin's *Process Model* and when asked whether there is a Japanese equivalent of this ground-breaking, but challenging, text he simply replied: 'Buddhism' (personal communication, July 2010).

Some of the points outlined here regarding mindful person-centred practice are illustrated in the case example that follows.

Mindfulness as person-centred practice: A case example (Alison Shoemark)

Enough, these few words are enough. If not these words, this breath.
   If not this breath, this sitting here … (Whyte, 1990, pp. 8–9)

The therapy with Theresa took place in a primary care counselling service based in the Counselling Research Clinic at the University of Abertay, Dundee. Clients to this service are referred from an inner-city GP practice, and receive open-ended counselling using an integrative approach that is described as a 'collaborative pluralistic framework for practice' (Cooper & McLeod, 2007). My practice, however, is person centred.

Theresa was a 35-year-old woman who presented with a tremendous fear of life-threatening illness and of not seeing her five-year-old son growing up. Her fear manifested in panic attacks and choking sensations. Theresa reported a significant change by the end of our work together, which was found to be sustained seven months later. At the start of each session, clients were invited to complete process measures (CORE: Clinical Outcome Routine Evaluation) and a Problem Rating Scale. The Problem Rating Scale is a scale of 0-9 (in response to the question 'How much has this problem been bothering you?'). A score of 9= 'couldn't be worse' and a score of 1= 'not bothering me at all'. The outcome data showed Theresa shift from a CORE score of 50 (on the border of mild/ moderate severity at the first interview), 44 at the start of session 2 to a score of 1 (healthy) at the start of session 5. Theresa's pattern of CORE responses was consistent with her verbal description of her symptoms. The problem rating shifted from a score of 9 at the start of therapy to 2 at session 5. At the 7-month follow-up her scores were CORE 4 and problem rating 2 (McLeod, 2008, case study materials).

The symptoms did not entirely disappear but she learned to live with them in a way that meant she had some control rather than the symptoms having control. The 'significant change' manifested as a markedly more congruent way of being, in which she was more accepting of and empathic towards herself and experiencing vastly reduced symptoms of panic. In essence, her life got better and she felt better. The process of change began in session 1, with Theresa introducing the metaphor of a 'box' to put 'things' into. In subsequent sessions she spoke at length and at depth about the deaths in her family. Prior to this, these experiences had not been recognized as particularly significant and, because of the family 'rules' of not causing upset to anyone, she could not articulate or express her fears.

The work with Theresa has already been closely scrutinized through a research process using the 'Ward' method (McLeod et al., 2008; Schielke et al., 2009). The working together of the three-member research team, John McLeod, Kate Smith and Alison Shoemark created a rich environment for discussion and professional development (McLeod et al., 2009). What follows will not be a definitive account of the research process but rather an attempt to explore and share the ebb and flow of the interactions between my client and myself and the way in which being mindful informs my person-centred counselling work. My process notes, session transcripts and personal session reflections support the account.

The directions I choose and those that particularly influence my life view inevitably influence my counselling practice. The principles of mindfulness that weave through this account illuminate my work with Theresa.

Mindfulness, like person-centred therapy, is not a goal-orientated approach. It is one that holds certain attitudes, attitudes that will weave through my work with Theresa. It means being curious, in this context that means engaging in an exploration into the 'how?' and 'what?' of her experience rather than the 'why?'; not judging, rather bringing an attitude of friendly interest that by its very nature precludes judgment; being patient and helping

Theresa to recognise things can only happen in their own time; non-striving – explicitly *not* trying to fix problems; staying present and acknowledging the arising and passing of experience – and the potential for clarity that comes with that. All of these attitudinal qualities can be said both to be deliberately cultivated by and to spontaneously arise from mindfulness practice.

The counselling process
(Client and counsellor words quoted directly from the five sessions will be indicated by italics.)

We are at the beginning of our relationship. I am quite nervous because I know Theresa has panic attacks and I fear I will be asked to offer a behavioural solution. I have no confidence I will succeed. I know all of this and have to work hard to recognise how inadequate I feel and resolve to simply meet Theresa and see how we go.

Theresa tells me she is experiencing almost constant panic attacks, choking and feeling as if she is dying; she is overwhelmed with anxiety that spreads to her little boy. She can't let him out of her sight. Her anxiety is affecting her relationship with her partner. She has a good social life, but that is also being adversely affected. Essentially she is living in and from her anxiety and panic, completely consumed by it, constantly judging herself.

I am aware of a dissonance, conscious of not becoming consumed by her anxiety or, indeed, my own. Thankfully, I don't have a sense that I need to *do* anything, although I think Theresa might be disappointed because she is desperate for reassurance and 'cure'; for things to be back to 'normal'.

I am, however, still thinking 'I can't do this. I can't help someone with panic attacks.' I realized, on reflection, that I have been presented with a diagnosis, not a person, and I have never set out to effect a cure of anything, let alone a person.

One of the potentially contradictory paradoxes of mindfulness and person-centered therapy is that: simply standing alongside the situation allows greater insight or awareness of it. So, as I do that, I clear space for myself, and see Theresa in a clearer light, less dominated by anxiety, ill health and panic.

Theresa talks more and in depth about the things that matter in her life, the idyllic family she grew up in and, bit by bit, death and her experience of it. She begins with her father and works back to the death of both her grandmothers, her experience of postnatal depression when she was sure her baby would die, all of the deaths dramatic and ranging back to when she was in her late teens, with no resources to do anything other than get on with it.

We are in session 2 now and, as I listen and she talks, I find myself sitting on the floor beside her, to hear better, as she is sobbing and her words quiet. I can see here how I move from a limiting aspect of my self concept ('I don't do panic attacks') to getting out of the way of myself and being completely alongside her.

In supervision I share a worry that this might not be working, that I am not really feeling a connection between us. My supervisor seems puzzled, as this is unusual for me. However, I realise I am striving to be a 'good' person-centred counsellor but getting stuck with my own feeling of inadequacy. I am still holding an attachment to the anxiety I began with and am questioning the meaning of 'relationship'. Through a process of honest self reflection, I realise that I am looking to build a relationship and she just wants to feel better! As I reflect, it comes to me like a bolt of lightening that the session we have just had held a kind of intimacy that goes way beyond words and this is what relationship is about: relational depth (Mearns and Cooper, 2005) – a real meeting at depth that, with hindsight, held what was necessary for Theresa to begin to make personal changes. A deeply accepting, compassionate space, with no judgment and vitally, not just from me to her, but from her to herself.

In the next session we focus on how emotional pain manifests in her. It is clear the panic attacks are already getting better, without us having talked about them in any great depth, without having looked at 'managing' them. Ultimately, both in person centered counselling and in mindfulness, this would be about 'knowing' rather than understanding; about an experiential phenomenological process – a visceral, heartfelt, body-centered way of appreciation. For Theresa, being curious about what her body was telling her through the physical manifestations of panic and choking sensations and learning to listen to it was crucial: '*it's like your body or your mind does things actually... so that you can cope'.*

As we move on, Theresa is having better weeks with far fewer panic attacks. She talks a lot about her father and about her birth family, about its 'idyllic' nature, where no emotions were expressed other than 'good' ones and where nothing happened to upset anyone. We talk about her wish to provide a home like she had as a child, '*we were so happy*', '*never argued*'. She is beginning to realise how she was clinging to childhood memories, how her relationship with G, her partner, was different – but still good. She relates to the interaction between mind and body, questioning her emotions, her experience of post natal depression and current experiences, being curious, asking '*could the mind be sore ... how can it show pain?*' And '*Is it all linked?*'

In essence, I too am offering 'gentle curiosity' (Segal, Williams and Teasdale, p. 228). I am curious and interested in how all these things that are going on for her are affecting her, but I have no need to make a judgment. So, importantly, negative experiencing is not pushed away, but rather we are standing together and I am encouraging her to 'turn towards and be with'. By doing this I am supporting her to develop a different relationship with her experience, enabling perhaps, a part of her to also watch with 'gentle curiosity'. I am sharing a way that I am with myself.

Being alongside Theresa, and, through my expression of empathy and acceptance, saying that the way it seems for me is that '*your head hurts*', '*your soul hurts*', '*you've opened the box and been in that dark place*' enables Theresa to go through a kind of 'rite of passage'(researcher reflection). 'The box' was a metaphor that Theresa used in the first session and was one that held a significant place throughout. She talked about putting things in a box: '*So it's like, like a little box, you know, tidy up and put it away*'. My response was: '*the lid is on but it pops open very easily*'. In effect, this opening of the box enables Theresa to move away from 'the familiar emotion terms' that Purton describes as necessary for therapeutic change (2004, p. 133; quoted above). Theresa reflects that she feels '*met in some way*'.

Throughout our work together I am offering the challenge of acceptance; inevitably then perhaps we both become more congruent. Self-acceptance and compassion are critical functions of the person-centered approach and of mindfulness. Both are crucial in order to facilitate the client's process. I am conscious of how far I have come from my initial anxiety about the content and the diagnosis Theresa arrived with and how far she has come – essentially, she has begun to learn to accept that this is how she is.

She tries to catch herself before the panic takes over. If it does, she reflects that '*it will not stay like this*'.

Together we have found a 'way of being' that is congruent, welcoming of experience and with space to wait and see what unfolds. By session 5 Theresa has made new rules for herself: '*don't waste time worrying*', '*the throat thing is in my mind*'. She has found an acceptance that says '*it's not surprising that I felt the way I did, given the experiences I had*'. She can acknowledge her experiencing, '*the way I am*'. She recognizes that the old coping strategy doesn't work, '*I can't fight it*'. It is the mindfulness paradox – embracing whilst observing – thus opening up opportunities for acceptance, insight and choice.

Conclusion

> In the beginner's mind there are many possibilities, but in the expert's there are few. (Suzuki, 2005, p. 1)

Eastern understanding needs to complement Western perspectives that have hitherto shaped the theory and practice of the person-centred approach to date. Mindfulness enables a deeper, essentially phenomenological, level of therapeutic acceptance and a manifestation of congruence that includes the experiencing of process through the felt sense. There is much to be learnt about mindfulness from Buddhism, as there is much to be learnt from Kabat-Zinn and those who have introduced and explained MBSR and MBCT programmes to Western cultures. From within the approach, the theory and practice of focusing offer both a practical means and theoretical insight into how mindfulness can actually work within our own practice. In this respect, an excellent starting point is Campbell Purton's *Person-Centred Therapy: the Focusing-Oriented Approach* (2004). However, mindfulness requires, above all, a freshness and a willingness to let go of rigidity, to be present to what 'is' and that is down to the individual and their ability to adopt 'a condition of complete simplicity' that exists prior to the thoughts, feelings and theories by which we may define ourselves.

My experience in relation to mindfulness
(Judy Moore)

I first learned about mindfulness as part of Buddhism from Campbell Purton in the early 1980s. It was not until I began my person-centred training in 1985 that I began to understand mindfulness as a practice that I could engage in and that could directly impact on my life.

A key influence for me in this respect was Alison, who I met on the course, the first PCT (Person-Centred Therapy) training. I was, at the time, teaching in adult education, compiling indexes, and finishing a PhD. On a personal level I was affected more than I probably realised by the early deaths of both my parents. A significant consolation over years had been literature and the empathic understanding that I found in the words of others who could express with great eloquence what I could not express, opening up possibilities of a much richer world of meaning. Meeting Alison, and forming a deep friendship with her, opened me up to a world where I could be in touch with the reality not only of the pain of life but also the joy that comes from being open and alive. We explored meditation together and I learned much from Alison's grounded, deeply acceptant way of being, her trusting of herself and her own experiencing. Alison embodied what I 'knew' at some level, just as T.S. Eliot (and others) wrote what I 'knew'.

Throughout the two and a half years of our training and in the years that followed I visited various Buddhist groups and learned different styles of meditation. In the early 1990s I joined a Soto Zen Buddhist group and have practised Soto Zen meditation since then. This form of meditation is based on being with what 'is', not simply the reality of ordinary daily life at a practical level, but also with the reality of inner experiencing at the level of the felt sense. Through the influence of Campbell Purton, the theory and practice of focusing have played an increasingly important part in my life and I qualified as a Focusing Trainer in 2003.

I have worked at the University of East Anglia since 1985, first as a trainee, then as a qualified counsellor and now as director both of the Counselling Service and the Centre for Counselling Studies, the latter of which was founded in 1992 by Brian Thorne. In the midst of a very demanding working life, I know that I owe much of my sanity to Soto Zen meditation. It has helped me to be more acceptant of myself and also helps me to give attention to simple, practical things, like cooking and gardening, which ground me in the here and now and make me look at the world around me with fresh, appreciative eyes.

My experience in relation to mindfulness
(Alison Shoemark)

Start where you are. (Pema Chödrön, 2005)

I can't begin to write about my own journey without first acknowledging the part Judy has played in supporting me and my practice, really being the motivation for my spiritual journey. We met on our counsellor training course in 1985 and, although we don't actually meet very often, the connection that was made during our training course has stayed quietly and strongly present. My person-centred training was a life changing experience and the journey towards self-acceptance and congruence that began there continues and is further defined through mindfulness practice.

So, this particular journey began 25 years ago when, I was introduced to poetry and the work of T.S. Eliot and in particular, Little Gidding:

> A condition of complete simplicity
> (Costing not less than everything)
> And all shall be well and
> All manner of thing shall be well ...

Not particularly to do with mindfulness per se, but the notion of 'complete simplicity' drew me in and the 'all shall be well' message touched some deep part of me.

The beginning of mindfulness is very difficult to define. Like being person centred it kind of crept up on me during my nursing training. After my training I focused on cancer nursing, working in a hospice and then in the community as a Macmillan nurse; ultimately it was this job that brought me to person-centred counselling and subsequently to a conscious embracing of mindfulness.

Having the experience of sudden death, recognising 'now' is all we have, became the foundation of my work. I used the practice to help me to be in the here and now, supporting people to use this available moment to say the things they needed/wanted to say, to be the way they wanted to be. Then it began to sink in that this was not only about other people – this was also about me! During, and for many years after, my counsellor training I went to various meditation groups and, noticing that I was finding a more peaceful and less stressed way of being, I developed my own way of meditating: weeding the garden, washing dishes, raking little Zen gardens, moving stones. Doing what I was doing because that was the thing to do, not thinking ahead about what next; bringing a quieter, more genuine quality to my life.

I have, more recently, had the opportunity to take various mindfulness courses. I found a way to revisit my person-centred origins through meditation, movement and body awareness; deepening my already fundamental approach of accepting what is being experienced in the moment, being curious but not judging, differentiating between experiences in the body, emotions and thoughts. These courses, and the associated focus on practice served to ground me in my meditation practice, take me further on my understanding of compassion and acceptance, which, in turn, has enhanced the person-centred quality of my counselling practice and teaching.

Acknowledgements
We want to end this chapter by acknowledging the acceptance, challenge and support we had during our training, and over the past twenty-five years, from our original tutors, Elke Lambers, Dave Mearns, and Brian Thorne, who have all influenced us, probably more than they know. In addition, we want to acknowledge John McLeod, who was part of our original training group, and with whom we are both particularly pleased to have continuing contact, for his approachability and incredible generosity in sharing of his ideas and writing. The influence and inspiration of Campbell Purton, another fellow trainee, is present throughout this chapter.

References

Bazzano, M (2010). Mindfulness in context. *Therapy Today, 21*(3), 32–6.

Chödrön, P (2005) *Start Where You Are.* London: Element (Harper Collins Publishers)

Cooper, M & McLeod, J (2007) A pluralistic framework for counselling and psychotherapy: Implications for research. *Counselling and Psychotherapy Research, 7*, 135–43.

Elias, D (2001) Compatible 'Ways of Being'?: A theoretical study of the compatibility of the person-centred approach and the Buddhist concept of mindfulness. Unpublished MA dissertation, University of Liverpool.

Geller, S (2003) Becoming whole: A collaboration between experiential psychotherapies and mindfulness meditation. *Person-Centered and Experiential Psychotherapies, 2*(4), 258–73.

Gendlin, E (1997a) *Experiencing and the Creation of Meaning: A philosophical and psychological approach to the subjective.* Evanston, IL: Northwestern University Press.

Gendlin, E (1997b) *A Process Model.* New York: The Focusing Institute.

Jiyu-Kennett, P (1999) *Zen is Eternal Life.* Mount Shasta, CA: Shasta Abbey Press.

Kabat-Zinn, J (1996) *Full Catastrophe Living: How to cope with stress, pain and illness using mindfulness meditation.* London: Piaktus.

Kabat-Zinn, J (2005) *Coming to our Senses: Healing ourselves and the world through mindfulness.* London: Piaktus.

Kabat-Zinn, J, Wheeler, E, Light, T, Skillings, A, Scharf, M, Cropley, T, Hosmer, D & Bernhard, J (1998) Influence of mindfulness-based stress reduction intervention on rates of skin clearing in patients with moderate to severe psoriasis undergoing phototherapy (UVB) and photochemotherapy (PUVA). *Psychosomatic Medicine, 60*, 625–32.

Ling, T (1981) *The Buddha's Philosophy of Man.* London: Everyman.

MacPhillamy, D (2003) *Buddhism from Within: An intuitive introduction to Buddhism.* Mt. Shasta, CA: Order of Buddhist Contemplatives.

Madigan, K (2006) Heal thyself/healthy self-mindfulness based approaches and person-centred approaches: A comparison. Unpublished dissertation, UEA, Norwich.

McLeod, J (2008) Case study materials. Unpublished notes.

McLeod, J, McLeod, J, Shoemark, A & Cooper, M (2008) Clients' criteria for evaluating the outcome of counselling in primary care. Paper presented at the British Association for Counselling and Psychotherapy Annual

Research Conference, Cardiff, May, and the International Society for Psychotherapy Research Annual Conference, Barcelona, June.

McLeod, J, McLeod, J & Shoemark, M (2009) A systematic case study research in counselling and psychotherapy: Using a team-based approach. Paper delivered to the Annual Research Conference of the British Association for Counselling and Psychotherapy, Portsmouth, 16th May.

Mearns, D (1997) *Person-Centred Counselling Training.* London: Sage.

Mearns, D & Cooper, M (2005) *Working at Relational Depth in Counselling and Psychotherapy.* London: Sage.

Moore, J (2004) Letting go of who I think I am: Listening to the unconditioned self. *Person-Centered and Experiential Psychotherapies, 3*(2),117–28.

Nhat Hanh, T (1993) *Transformation and Healing: Sutra on the four establishments of mindfulness.* London: Rider.

Purton, C (2004) *Person-Centred Therapy: The focusing-oriented approach.* Basingstoke: Palgrave Macmillan.

Schielke, H, Fishman, J, Osatuke, K & Stiles, W (2009) The ward method: Creative consensus on interpretations of qualitative data. *Psychotherapy Research, 19*(4 & 5), 558–65.

Segal, Z, Williams, J & Teasdale, J (2002) *Mindfulness-Based Cognitive Therapy for Depression: A new approach to preventing relapse.* New York: Guilford Press.

Suetake, Y (2010) The clinical significance of Gendlin's process model. *Person-Centered and Experiential Psychotherapies, 9*(2), 118–27.

Suzuki, S (2005) *Zen Mind, Beginner's Mind.* New York: Shambala Publications.

Tolle, E (2005) *The Power of Now: A guide to spiritual enlightenment.* London: Hodder and Stoughton.

Van der Kooy, A & McEvenue, K (2006) Focusing with your whole body: A CD integrated wholebody focusing learning program (CD). Privately printed: Marlborough, UK and Toronto.

Whyte, D (1990) *When Many Rivers Meet.* Langley, WA: Many Rivers Press.

6

Spirituality, Focusing and the Truth Beyond Concepts

Campbell Purton

Brian Thorne's work has for many years been concerned with themes that lie in the borderland between therapy and spirituality. In this chapter I want to take up one such theme: that of a reality which lies beyond concepts, but with which we can interact in ways that lead to new concepts and fuller living. The existence of such a reality seems to be to be central to the conception of the spiritual.

I begin with a few quotations from spiritual writings in the traditions of (respectively) Hinduism, Christianity, Zen, Sufism, Buddhism and Taoism.

> [The Brahman] cannot be defined by word or idea; as the Scripture says, it is the One before whom words recoil. (Shankara)

> As the Godhead is nameless, and all naming is alien to Him, so also the soul is nameless; for it is here the same as God. (Eckhart)

> Sixty-six times have these eyes beheld the changing scenes of autumn.
> I have said enough about moonlight, ask me no more.
> Only listen to the voice of pines and cedars, when no wind stirs.
> (Ryo-nen)

> Sell your cleverness and buy bewilderment;
> Cleverness is mere opinion, bewilderment is intuition. (Rumi)

> There is an unborn, an un-brought-to-being, an unmade, an unformed. If there were not, there would be no path to freedom

An earlier version of some of the material in this chapter was presented at a conference 'Spiritual Challenges in the 21st century' in Ditchingham, Norfolk, 8th–10th September, 2006.

made known here for one who is born, brought to being, made, formed. (Udana Sutra)

He who knows does not speak;
He who speaks does not know. (Lao Tsu)

The last quotation rather obviously confronts us with a paradox that seems inherent in all of them – Lao Tzu says that people who speak of the Tao do not *know* – but he is himself speaking of the Tao! We find a less paradoxical formulation in the Buddhist *Lankavatara Sutra* :

With the lamp of word and discrimination one must go beyond word and discrimination, and enter upon the path of realisation.

This suggests that rather than lapsing into silence, we can still use words, but that they need to be used in a special way, a way that perhaps can *point at* a more-than-conceptual reality, or help us to interact with it, rather than – *too* paradoxically – trying to formulate it in concepts.

The central theme that I will be concerned with is that there is a 'truth beyond concepts', that this truth is more important than our conceptual truths, and that it can in some ways provide us with a guide in formulating our view of the world, and in trying to live better lives.

This is a spiritual, and indeed mystical, view of things, which appeals to some people more than others. Such a view of things would be rejected by many people, and I am interested in the question of whether there are sound arguments in its favour. The question of justification seems important because commitment to the view has important implications for our lives, some of which I will discuss later. Are there useful things that can be said in debate with those who are sceptical about it? Can we use words to lead beyond words?

In his book *The Measure of Things* (2002) David Cooper, Professor of Philosophy at the University of Durham, suggests that a mystical view of reality is the only plausible way out of the current impasse in philosophy – the impasse between traditional objective views of the world on the one hand, and post-modernist social-constructionist views on the other. Effective philosophical arguments tend to be lengthy, as they need to address all the potential objections that can be raised against one's position, and Cooper's argument is no exception. His is a lengthy book, but I think the essence of the argument can be stated fairly briefly.

Consider first the group of thinkers we can call objectivists, absolutists, or traditionalists. They argue that in religion, as well as in science, we seek truth. They insist that there is a reality 'out there' to which our ideas are answerable. The earth really does move around the sun, and it really is wrong to be cruel to animals. These are, if you like, brute facts. Of course, we don't know the whole truth in either science or morality, and maybe we only know only a tiny bit. (Isaac Newton said "I do not know what I may appear to the world; but to myself I seem to have been only like a boy playing on the seashore, and diverting myself in now and then finding a smoother pebble or a prettier shell than ordinary, whilst the great ocean of truth lay all undiscovered before me.") And even when we do think that we have discovered something true we may come to see that we have been mistaken. Nevertheless there *is* the truth and the good at which we aim. Science makes progress, we discover more and more as the years go by. In morality progress may be more dubious – but this just means that we need to put more effort into determining what really is valuable. The essential point is that there *is* a reality, and it is there independently of us. The laws of aerodynamics are what they are – if we ignore them then our planes won't fly. On this kind of view, the truth is not *beyond* concepts, it is just difficult and time-consuming to find concepts that adequately formulate the truth.

Proponents of this view argue that we need the notion of a truth external to us if we are not to live in an unreal world derived from our whims and fancies. We need to acknowledge that there is a reality which, sooner or later, we will bump up against, and we need to adapt to it. We need to have a degree of humility before the world. We didn't construct the world – the world constructed us. In short, the reality of the world is not beyond concepts – rather, our concepts, insofar as they are good concepts, bring us into contact with the actual structure of the world.

Another aspect of the same point is that we need a sense of what is there independently of us if we are to make any assessment of our lives, if we are to make any sound judgements about what is true or good. It is not enough to say 'This is good by the standards of my society, or 'It is good by my standards that I have chosen.' For the standards I have chosen, or the standards of my society may not be good standards. To do what is right in terms of certain standards that are themselves not right, is *not* to do what is right. To be serious about one's judgements one must believe that there are standards independent of oneself. There has to be something outside oneself that one tries to live up to. One tries, or at least hopes, that one can bring one's life a bit more into line with what is, independently of one's current ideas and wishes, true and good. That is a very brief sketch of the absolutist position.

A quite different position is taken by people we can call relativists, postmodernists, or social constructionists: for them, there *is* no world independent of human beings, and human concepts. What we call 'the world' is a social construction. *Our* world is very different from the world of the ancient Greeks, or the world of contemporary traditional people in New Guinea. The world view of science – in particular – is one possibility among many. It is a good (in the sense of 'useful') view insofar as one is mainly interested in predicting and controlling things. But like any conceptual scheme it is relative to its purposes, and these are *human* purposes The scientific view of things is just one view – it is how the world is for certain people, for certain purposes. Most of us have grown up in it and take it for granted, just as is the case for any culture. But there is no world *just there*, independently of languages and cultural forms. There is no reality independent of human reality (the social construction point), and there are many different human realities (the relativistic point). We need to recognise this, so that we don't impose our way of seeing things on other people. We need a kind of humility in connection with our own views. They are not the only possibility. That is a very brief sketch of the relativist position.

The two contemporary positions can be summarised as:

1. Absolutists: That there is a world there independent of us, which has its own structure that we need to learn about and adapt to.

2. Relativists: There is no world independent of us – we need to accept that everything is relative to our culture. What we take

to be objective facts are human constructions. We need to accept and live with this relativity of truth.

The dilemma in a nutshell is that the positions are incompatible, yet each side has a strong case to make:

1. Absolutists: We need to make assessments of our lives and of the world, and for that to be possible there need to be objective standards by which we can make our assessments and by which we can judge our culture's beliefs and practices.

2. Relativists: Any stateable or conceptualised standard exists only within a cultural context. There can't be absolute standards, standards that are independent of particular societies.

Even more briefly: the objectivists are right that there needs to be a reality outside us, but the relativists are right that any reality of which we can speak is conceptually culture-bound, and so *not* outside us.

The dilemma may seem irresolvable, but as David Cooper points out, there is the possibility of a way through. The source of standards, or the ultimate reality to which our ideas are answerable, is only culture-relative if it has to be describable or articulated or conceptualised. But there are many traditions in which the ultimate reality is held to be *beyond* concepts. I referred to such traditions at the beginning. For them the ultimate reality is not conceptualised but 'pointed at' with phrases such as 'the Unborn' 'the ground of our being', 'the Tao', 'the Void', 'Brahman'. It could be objected that these are themselves concepts, but that is not obviously true. These terms seem to work not by conceptualising but by 'pointing' to something. It is not as if one could spell out what exactly something would have to be in order to count as being 'the Tao'. In Heidegger's terms one is pointing not at any particular beings, but at Being itself.

Suppose one *can* point in this way – then there can be an absolute reality which we bump up against and to which we are answerable (as the absolutists require), but this reality that is indeed 'just there' cannot be described in words or concepts. Hence it is not open to the objection of the humanist–relativists that anything which can be expressed must be expressed in terms of some particular conceptual scheme. This reality is a truth, but it is a truth beyond concepts.

An example from the history of science may help to make it clearer what such a 'truth' might involve. In Aristotle's scheme of things a heavy object such as a stone falls to the ground because it is constituted largely by the element of earth, and the natural place for earthy things is at the centre of the world. Similarly, firey things such as sparks, rise up towards the circumference of the world. If you lived in the middle ages you would see a stone as seeking the centre of the world when you dropped it. Then with the beginnings of modern science in the seventeenth century we encounter a different conception of what happens when the stone is dropped. According to Newton all particles of matter attract each other with a gravitational force, and the falling stone is seen as being attracted by the gravitational field of the Earth. This is probably how most people see the event today. Then in the twentieth century there arose a different conception again: According to Einstein the stone is simply following its natural path in a curved space-time continuum. And in a few hundred years time, no doubt, there will be further and still different conceptions. Now what *really* makes the stone fall? A physicist who is an absolutist will today give Einstein's account. Most non-physicists today will, if they are absolutists, probably give Newton's account, since that is the one that has most effectively penetrated common-sense thinking and school textbooks. But these absolutist views are implausible, just because *there are alternatives.* On the other hand, it is also implausible to say that there is no definite reason why the stone falls, that falling stones are social constructions and that you can think about them any way you like.

But there is a third option. According to this we should say that there is indeed something that makes the stone fall. It is *that which is formulated in different ways* by Aristotle, Newton, Einstein and possible future scientists. The *something* that is formulated in different ways is the reality. It is beyond concepts in the sense that it cannot be fully formulated in any particular set of concepts; rather, it is what gives the concepts the limited effectiveness which they do have. This 'something' is absolutely real, and it is experienced as we drop the stone. How we conceptualise the situation depends on our cultural context, but there is an important sense in which our situation and our experience of it is not culture-relative. It is this experience and situation which can be formulated in different ways in different cultures.

The same sort of account, I think, is relevant in connection with explanations of human behaviour. It is not the oedipus complex, or the archetype, or the introjection that is the reality. These are conceptual formulations which have their value, and may draw attention to various aspects of a person's situation, but what actually gives rise to the behaviour is *that which is formulated in these different ways in the different conceptual systems.* That 'something' is immediately experienced – it might be felt by the person involved as a heavy constraint, for example. There is *something there*, which is conceptualised by different psychologies in different ways.

Suppose then that we can make theoretical sense of an absolute reality that is beyond concepts. It may still be objected that such a notion is of little use in practice. In practice we always think within a particular conceptual scheme. What is the point of adding that beyond any scheme is something non-conceptual? How can something non-conceptual have any significant impact on what we are to believe or value? How can this doctrine of 'emptiness' – to use the Buddhist terminology – tell us anything about what the world is like, or how we should live?

There are two ways of approaching that question. One is to draw out the general theoretical implications of the idea of a more-than-conceptual reality; the other is to draw attention to *practices* in which engagement with the more-than-conceptual can lead to changes both in concepts and in ways of living.

General theoretical implications of a more-than-conceptual reality

David Cooper points out that a doctrine of the inexpressible Absolute, or a doctrine of 'mystery', as he calls it, *does* have general implications for how we see the world and how we should live. The doctrine is not compatible, for example, with seeing the world as *ultimately* a physical system specifiable in terms of the concepts of physics and chemistry. For scientific purposes the world *can* be seen in that way, but according to the doctrine of mystery, this is not ultimately how things are. The doctrine of mystery entails that the scientific view of things is just one view, and this has implications for how we see science. There are signs that an insight of this sort is already beginning to dawn. For example, the British Psychological Society now has a section devoted to transpersonal psychology, there is a department of parapsychology at Edinburgh University, and at the 2006 British Association meeting in Norwich there was, for the first time, an afternoon at which people with 'heretical' views were given their say.

Then again, the doctrine of mystery is incompatible with any view of human beings which reduces people to that which can be accommodated within some conceptual scheme, whether Freudian, Marxist, theological, biological or whatever. People, and the world, are *beyond* any scheme. This is not to deny that schemes can be helpful, but it is to say that there is an inexpressible 'more' to things. The current emphasis in institutions on trying to make everything explicit in terms of mission statements, targets, performance criteria and so on is something which the doctrine of mystery would tend to question. There is of course a place for making things explicit, but the danger is that the explicit formulations become mistaken for what is really there. Instead of trying to get a sense – largely implicit – of what the *situation* requires, the current tendency is to operate in terms of what the *criteria* require. In other words our society tends to see everything in technological and managerial terms which specify ends and means, but such technological thinking is only one kind of approach, which in many situations, according to the doctrine of mystery, is inappropriate.

To take a different sort of example, if we accept the doctrine of mystery then it becomes important to try to attune ourselves to what William James in *The Varieties of Religious Experience* called the 'more', to that which lies 'beyond' (James 1902/1985, pp. 457–8). But some styles of life seem incompatible with such attunement, e.g., life-styles in which all one's attention is devoted to specific plans and ambitions, a 'busy-busy' sort of life. The doctrine suggests, at least, that we need to build into our lives periods of not being busy, of times when we allow ourselves to be open to the 'more', periods of something like meditation or prayer.

Then there are certain contemporary attitudes which seem very much bound up with a technological and utilitarian view of things, such as our way of treating animals. Factory-farming methods seem hardly compatible with an openness to the *reality of the animal*, a reality that goes beyond our limited conception of it as a source of food for ourselves.

So, perhaps surprisingly, the doctrine of mystery, the doctrine that the reality of things lies beyond concepts, can have direct implications for how we should think of the world and how we should treat it. In other words it provides at least the outline for an ethics. However, we need to be careful here. The doctrine should make us wary of ethical *systems and rules*. By its nature, the doctrine cannot specify explicit *rules* for what we should do in particular situations. For example it could not possibly specify that we should be vegetarians. Rather, it by its nature points at the reality of things, a reality that is independent of our desires – and awaits our response.

An important aspect of this view is that concepts can only express limited aspects of reality – there is always 'more'. This point also has immediate ethical implications. There *is* such a thing as the conceptual expression of reality, and much human accomplishment depends on that. On the other hand we can become trapped in the conceptual, rather than using it as a gateway to what is 'more'. William Blake says:

> He who binds to himself a joy
> Does the wingèd life destroy;
> But he who kisses the joy as it flies
> Lives in eternity's sunrise.

The 'binding' or 'fixing' possibility is inherent in human life. Human consciousness conceptualises, makes forms, but this conceptualising capacity is a two-edged sword.

We can easily take the forms, the distinctions, too seriously, and lose touch with what is *beyond* forms. The difficulty (and the power) of concepts is that they specify precisely how things are, and how they are not. They *limit* reality in specified ways. From a conceptual scheme much follows about how things must or must not be done, about what is possible and what is not possible. However, the *musts* and *shoulds* are always relative to that particular scheme, and no particular scheme can be identified with the truth of things.

The doctrine of mystery does not encourage us to abandon all forms, but to hold them lightly. Carl Rogers (1959, p. 191) suggested that a theory is best seen as 'a fallible, changing attempt to construct a network of gossamer threads that will contain the solid facts'. Yet we may feel a concern here. If we hold on to the forms only lightly, if our concepts are but 'gossamer threads', then will we end up being open to a multitude of foolish views, and to a toleration of what should not be tolerated? How does the doctrine of mystery fit with commitment to values? Does it allow for things to which we need to hold firmly, and *not* lightly? Should we not hold firmly to the value of such things as courage, temperance, patience, unselfishness, generosity?

What I would suggest is that the doctrine of mystery involves holding firm to the 'mystery' itself, that is, to the whole, to our felt sense of what is best – when we take everything into account. The traditional virtues, such as courage and generosity can then be seen to follow from this. For example, courage can be seen as a matter of holding to what is sensed as a whole to be good – taking everything into account – *in spite of one's fears*. Temperance similarly could be seen as a matter of not taking one's desires too seriously in comparison with one's sense of the overall good. Patience would be a matter of sensing that there is the larger picture in which you don't *have to* have this *now*. From this perspective, the various virtues fall out from consideration of the various ways in which we might not follow our overall felt sense of what is good, but instead take too seriously particular desires or aversions.

Something that we tend to take *very* seriously is the feeling of *myself* as distinct from *others*. We not only make the distinction, as we must, but hang a huge emotional weight on it. It seems to matter enormously whether it is *I* or whether it is *you* to whom the doctor is referring when he says that a painful operation is going to be essential. Schopenhauer writes that '...the better person is the one who makes least difference between himself and others, and does not regard them as absolutely non-ego; whereas to the bad person this difference is great, in fact absolute.' (Schopenhauer, 1844; translation in Payne, 1974, p. 507). It seems clear that holding tightly to the distinction between oneself and others, or holding tightly to one's concept of oneself, is another example of valuing concepts or forms more than that from which they arise, and that holding to the distinction or concept less tightly will promote generosity, fairness, and kindness, and a sense of the equality of all. Hence perhaps arise the Christian precept of 'loving one's neighbour as oneself' and the Buddhist notion of the unreality of oneself as an entity independent of one's interactions with others.

It is worth noting that the ethical principle that emerges here is that other people are of *equal* value to oneself, not of *more* value. Kierkegaard (1847; translation Hong, 1962, pp. 35–6) drew attention to the way in which the Christian commandment to 'love your neighbour as yourself' might appear to be inferior to romantic expressions of loving another person *more* than oneself, but he argued that the sort of love celebrated by the romantic poet is in fact self-love.

Of course it might be said that since we are so strongly biased in favour of ourselves it can do no harm to recommend an over-balance in the opposite direction, and in earlier times there may have been something to be said for this. However, in our contemporary culture it seems that such an intensification of the commandment is likely to be dangerous. In our culture, as the counsellor finds almost every day, there are many people who do not value *themselves*. This seems to be an unprecedented situation – I have heard Buddhist teachers from Tibet express bafflement over it. The Buddhist teachings, like the Christian teachings, are for the most part geared up to the assumption that people love themselves, and need help in loving others to the same extent. But in the modern world the teaching may, for some people, have to modified to become 'love yourself as your neighbour'! Either way round, what is needed still follows from the principle that one should try to sense what is needed in the situation as a whole, and not take oneself (or one's neighbour) *too* seriously.

Relating to the more-than-conceptual reality

Reference to what we discover in counselling brings me to the second approach to the question of how a more-than-conceptual reality can tell us something about what the world is like, and how to live. The first approach – through developing the logical consequences of the view – told us something in general terms about how we need to think and act if we are not to alienate ourselves from the reality of what lies beyond concepts. But these general principles cannot be regarded as a system of rules. And in any case no general principle is ever sufficient in practice – we also need to know how to apply the principles in particular situations. (What would count as being generous in *this* peculiar situation? What would it be to treat someone like *this* as if they were me?) What is needed is a method of attuning ourselves to what the situation requires in all its fullness. Any situation is indefinitely complex, and – according to the doctrine of mystery – it cannot be fully specified in a conceptual way. Once a situation *is* specified in a particular way, *then* we can use logic and moral principles to guide us in what we should do. But the doctrine of mystery requires us to think about the situation on a level that goes deeper than our concepts. We need to approach the situation in a more-than-conceptual way, to think about it beyond concepts. For many people the notion of thinking beyond concepts will not make any sense, but it is indeed possible. We can see such thinking taking place in artistic creation for example, and also in counselling and psychotherapy.

If we begin to move beyond concepts, if we approach what the theologian Rudolf Otto called the *mysterium*, where will we come to? Otto (1917/1958, p. 13) says:

> Conceptually, *mysterium* denotes merely that which is hidden and esoteric, that which is beyond conception or understanding, extraordinary and unfamiliar. The term does not define the object more positively in its qualitative character. But though what is enunciated in the word is negative, what is meant is something absolutely and intensely positive. This pure positive we can experience in feelings, feelings which our discussion can help us to make clear to us, in so far as it arouses them actually in our hearts.

Going beyond concepts does not leave us nowhere. It leaves us in the realm of what can be called 'feelings', but which is better expressed in Gendlin's term 'felt sense'.

'Felt sense' is a phrase introduced by Gendlin (1978/1991) as a way of referring to an aspect of our experiencing which is very easy to miss. The felt sense of a situation, or of a problem or of a work of art is not the specific feelings or emotions aroused in us, but the less obvious overall feel of the whole thing. For example, if we stand in front of a picture in an art gallery we may have all sorts of thoughts and feelings about the picture. But we can also pause, let these thoughts and feelings go by, and try to get an overall sense of the picture as a whole. It may take a few moments – perhaps half a minute – for this felt sense to form. If we ask *where* in the body are we sensing the picture the answer may not be obvious, but for many people a felt sense is experienced somewhere in the central part of the body, less often in the head or outer parts of the body. It is as if from the centre of the body we are experiencing what the picture centrally is for us. There may be no words that come to us by way of characterising the felt sense, or it may be that, after a minute or two, a word does come. Or, while keeping our attention on the felt sense, we can deliberately ask 'What is this?…what is the feel of this?' And a word may come, for example, 'wild', 'Indian', 'quaint', 'twisted-up'. Such words are hardly descriptions of the picture, but they come directly from the felt sense, and can help us to stay with it. It is easy to lose touch with a felt sense, but the associated words can bring it back to us. We say 'What was it that picture made me feel?... I've lost it... let me see... it was 'twisted-up'…. Ah yes, now I have it again… *that* feeling'.

The important point is that we can stay with and give attention to something as a whole. Doing this is different from thinking about it, or noticing what emotions one is feeling. Thoughts and emotions are more specific responses – the felt sense takes in the whole of the thing, and can in that way *include* many thoughts and emotions.

Now it is an interesting fact that in counselling sessions clients quite often give attention to their problems in this way. By the time a client has reached the counsellor's room they are probably fairly familiar with their thoughts and emotions surrounding the problem. But having thought and felt about it they are still stuck. In an effective counselling session what tends to happen is that the counsellor reflects what they say in a way that helps them to stay with their experiencing of their problem as a whole. In the safety and peace of the counselling session they can begin to get in touch with a sense of 'all that upsetting thing', and often from the felt sense new possibilities emerge.

The felt sense of a situation is non-conceptual because it is not an experience of a *kind* of thing. In this way it is unlike emotions. An emotion such as anger or pride is a kind or category of experiencing, and we can explain roughly *what* kind it is. For example anger is a response to some sort of violation, while pride is a feeling that something good has been done and *you* did it. In the experiencing of emotions concepts (classifications, kinds, forms) are already essentially involved; the experiencing is already parcelled up in particular ways, which to some extent are culture-relative. (For example no-one experiences piety in a culture where there are no gods or respect for the gods; no-one has a sense of family shame in a very individualistic culture). By contrast, the felt sense of a situation is the feeling of *that* situation; the felt sense may include or involve various emotions and conceptions, but it is not in itself conceptual. It is a feeling, or sense, of *all that.*

The important point now is that just as we can give attention to our perceptions, emotions and all the rest of our conceptually structured world, we can also give attention to our felt sense of our situation, of how our life is going, of what we should be doing. This takes practice, because we are so used to attending to specific aspects of our experiencing, and formulating what we experience in words and concepts. It is easy not to notice that in addition to all the detailed forms in our experience of a situation there is also the feel of the situation *as a whole.* Yet we can come to notice it. It is – in a special sense – a 'feeling', and it can often involve a distinctly bodily aspect such as feeling 'shaky', 'bubbly', 'wound-up'. These of course are general terms, but they stand at the boundary between what is formed and what lies beyond form. They convey something of how our body is responding to – 'that'. Through noticing the body-feel we may be able to hold on to our sense of – 'that'.

Gendlin and other writers (e.g. Gendlin, 1978/2003; Hinterkopf, 2008) have developed detailed instructions which can help one to interact with a felt sense in ways that allow new feelings and conceptions to arise from it. The felt sense is the experience of *that whole thing*, so that within it is all that is implicit within *that.* One's concepts, by contrast, select particular aspects or configurations of *that,* none of which can fully express all that is in *that.* Yet through giving attention to the felt sense new aspects or configurations can arise which help in understanding or dealing with the situation. It is as if when we give our attention to the felt sense, and gently try some simple questions such as 'What is this, really?' or 'What does this need?' the felt sense talks back. If we are quiet and wait for a few moments then often something will come – sometimes an image, or some words, or a new perspective on, or feel for, some aspect of the situation. Then the situation feels a little different, and we have a new felt sense. We check again, and again something may shift, or something new may again come to us. There is an ongoing interactive process here, something like a dialogue, and as we participate in this dialogue it can gradually become clearer how things stand, or what we should do.

This is the process which – in connection with psychotherapy – Gendlin called 'focusing'. But it is not essentially a therapeutic procedure. It can be used, or can happen naturally, in any kind of creative work, where one stays with an unclear felt sense of something and allows new forms to arise. Its importance, so far as the spiritual is concerned, is that it provides a clear and concrete example of how we can relate to a more-than-conceptual reality.

I suspect that what goes on in focusing is not very different from what goes on in certain traditional practices of prayer and meditation. Certainly I have found parallels in some forms of Buddhist meditation, such as dzogchen (Hookham 1992; Shikpo 2007) or mahamudra (Namgyal 1986). However, much more investigation is needed in that area. It has been noted by a number of writers that focusing is in some ways different from (at least some kinds of) meditation, and no doubt the same applies to prayer. What do seem to be common themes are that, first, we make reference to the idea of a more-than-conceptual reality – we can refer to it, even though we cannot describe it; and secondly, that there is the possibility of interacting with this reality in a way that can provide both novel conceptions of the nature of things, and guidance on how to carry our lives forward.

References

Cooper, DE (2002) *The Measure of Things: Humanism, humility and mystery.* Oxford: Clarendon Press.

Gendlin, ET (1978/2003) *Focusing* (Revised and updated edn). London: Rider.

Gendlin, ET (1991) Thinking beyond patterns. In: B den Ouden & M Moen (eds) *The Presence of Feeling in Thought* (pp. 21–151). New York: Peter Lang.

Hinterkopf, E (2008) *Integrating Spirituality in Counselling: A manual for using the experiential focusing method.* Ross-on-Wye: PCCS Books.

Hookham, M (1992) *Openness, Clarity, Sensitivity.* Oxford: Longchen Foundation.

Kierkegaard, S (1847/1962) *Works of Love* (H. Hong, Trans). New York: Harper & Row.

Namgyal, TT (1986) *Mahamudra: The quintessence of mind and meditation.* Boston: Shambhala.

Otto, R (1917/1958) *The Idea of the Holy* (J. Harvey, Trans). Oxford: Oxford University Press.

Rogers, CR (1959) A theory of therapy, personality and interpersonal relationships, as developed in the client-centered framework. In: S. Koch (ed) *Psychology: A study of a science, Vol 3: Formulations of the person and the social context* (pp. 184–256). New York: McGraw-Hill.

Schopenhauer, A (1844/1966) *The World as Will and as Representation,* Vol. II (EFJ Payne, Trans). New York: Dover Publications.

Shikpo, R (2007) *Never Turn Away: The Buddhist path beyond hope and fear.* Boston: Wisdom Publications.

7

The Person and Evil

Peter F. Schmid

Introduction

The anthropology of the Person-Centred Approach is rooted in the notion of personhood with both its substantial and its relational dimensions – a view of the human being that has been developed within the framework of occidental theology and philosophy. Among its main characteristics is the belief in the human's freedom of choice and responsibility. This understanding of the human as person implies the challenge of an authentic confrontation with and the necessity of taking a stance towards the phenomenological fact of what we call 'evil' and the 'dark or negative side' of human experience and behaviour. Asking ourselves who we really are and therefore how we best relate to each other – or the other way round! – has been triggering the challenging question about the nature of evil from the very beginning of our reflection upon ourselves. In this chapter I will follow some of the traces of this question in ontology, anthropology, theology, ethics, politics and individual and social psychology. I will discuss its implications and consequences for the place of 'the negative' in the therapeutic process based on an existential view of an encounter-oriented psychotherapy that truly deserves the name 'person-centred'.

This chapter is an enlarged and revised version based on an invited paper given at the symposium of APA, Division of Theoretical and Philosophical Psychology, 'Luminaries and Legacies: Carl Rogers and Rollo May', on the occasion of the APA Annual Convention, Toronto, 2009.

Unde malum?

Whence the evil?

Why have we been dealing with this question from time immemorial? It preoccupies us because of our experience, since the so called dark or negative side of nature, the human being included, puzzles us, makes us suffer, fascinates us. It is one of the questions that seem to be unanswerable and thus challenges us to ever new taking a stance. We can't get it out of our mind, no matter if we try to get to grips with nature by research or cope with human behaviour by trying to understand and empathise. We can't get it out of our doing even if we try to do our best. We can't get it out of our experiences even if we try to ignore it, to fight it or to keep cool. Even more after the outraged cruelties and tyrannies of the 20th century, after Auschwitz, Hiroshima, the Gulag Archipelago, after 9/11, in the face of the threat of a nuclear war or of worldwide terrorist attacks.

And why is this question important to psychotherapists and counsellors? There are two reasons. To understand the human nature – and even more: whether there is such thing as a human nature – is at stake as is the adequate practice of psychotherapy and counselling, pedagogy, social and pastoral work, etc. that comes as a consequence from our image of the human being.

Philosophy discerns, beginning with Plato, between the physical evil (illness, pain, ugliness, accidents, natural disasters; megalomania, delusion; structural evil, etc.), the metaphysical evil (i.e. Leibnitz' term for the imperfect world: finiteness, limits, death, etc.) and the moral or ethical evil (evil intentions and actions). Only the last and where it derives from is of interest here.

Two great humanistic authors, Rollo May and Carl Rogers, dealt with the problem and came to divergent positions which they expressed in their famous exchanges of statements (Rogers, 1981; 1982; May, 1982). On the basis of their views I will discuss the problem.

Rollo May spoke about 'angry, hostile, negative – that is evil – feelings of the clients' (1982, p. 245), 'violent rage or collective paranoia in time of war or compulsive sex or oppressive behaviour' (p.240), and 'destructive possession' (1969, p. 131). Rogers used the term for 'destructive, cruel, malevolent behaviour' (1981, p. 237);

religiously motivated terrorism, 'murderous impulses, desires to hurt, feelings of anger and rage, desires to impose our will on others' (1982, p. 254), 'the dark and often sordid side of life' (Rogers, 1958, p. 17).

I would not see anger or aggression as evil; these may be evil depending on the context, the givens, the motives. As a working definition to start with I use 'evil' for hostile, destructive, malevolent intentions and actions, such that cause suffering; in a word: anything that is 'against the good life'.

First I shall consider two fundamental philosophical and anthropological positions in the history of humankind and then have a closer look at May's and Rogers' stances. Thereafter I deal with the practical consequences for therapy. Next I am going check the resulting alternative 'being-centred or person-centred'? And finally I will try to sketch, how a genuinely *person*-centred and dialogical anthropology might comprehend what we call the evil.

Two fundamental positions

Among others – e.g., the pessimistic stance of Schopenhauer (that everything is evil) or the optimism of Leibnitz (that this is the best of all possible worlds) – there are two classical answers to the problem of moral evil: Either the evil is there from the beginning as a fundamental force in the universe as the opposite to the good *or* it is a deficiency of the good and has no being in itself. These positions characterise the essential difference between dualistic religions and world views and the monotheistic religions and such philosophies that believe in one sole source of all being.

It is worth noticing that the question discussed here is *whence the evil?*, not: *what is the evil?* Although these questions are of course interrelated, experiencing evil we ask: *why? whence? how come?* and *how to overcome?* And the corresponding ethical question has to be: *How do you deal with the evil? Which action do you take in the face of the phenomenon of evil? How do you respond to those persons that you experience as evil-minded or evil doing?* I do not want to speculate; I am dealing with a phenomenological issue of original experience.

Dualism: Good versus evil

Is the evil there from the beginning? An evil principle opposite to a good one? A good god and an evil god? A good law and an evil one that rule the world? This classical dualistic world view can be found e.g., in Parsism, in Manichaeism, Priscillianism and Gnosticism. In Zoroastrianism, the classical Persian religion of Zarathustra two fundamental principles compete: Ahura Mazda or Ormuz, the good god of creation and order, and Angra Manju or Ariman, the bad one, the god of lying, destruction and death. The human's free will decides between them and thus decides the fate of the cosmos. In Manichaeism and Neoplatonism the soul is the good and the body the evil principle.

Two principles that rule the world are in Heraklit's philosophy with the interplay of opposites, in Gnosticism (light vs darkness; 'soma sema' ['το μεν σωμα εστιν ημιν σημα'] – the body as grave for the soul) and Schelling's idea of the history as fight between light and darkness, good and evil. Two principles are, of course, the basis of Freud's (1920) metapsychology, developed after World War I: all human behavior and in fact all that exists is the result of the ongoing fight of libido and aggression, eros and thanatos, the drives of connection and union, enhancement and love on the one hand and destruction and death – today we might speak of entropy – on the other hand. The interior of the human being is the venue of this battle. In the development of the infant evil is everything that has to do with deprivation of love; later the evil became a generic term for any disturbance of living together by the human drive of aggression and self-destruction. For Freud this is not only a psychological, rather a meta-psychological cosmic reality: The goal of life is death; everything will end as inorganic matter, as it once was, before there was life; fossilisation is the perspective of redemption. (Safranski, 1999, p. 248)

Rollo May

Rollo May (1909 – 1994) also holds a dualistic position in postulating that the human's potentialities are 'the source *both* of our constructive and our destructive impulses'. (May, 1982, p. 240) This does not come as a surprise, if you take May's professional background in psychoanalysis into account. May, analysand of Erich Fromm, had attended seminars with the second founder of psychoanalysis, Alfred

Adler, in Vienna in the early 1930s, had worked as a psychoanalyst in private practice and his primary professional association was with the William Alanson White Institute of Psychiatry, Psychoanalysis and Psychology in New York from 1948 till 1975, the year of his move to California (Kirschenbaum and Henderson, 1989, pp. 229–30). Despite his big leap from conventional analysis and its mode of therapy towards existentialism and humanistic stances his basic convictions are obviously influenced by psychoanalytical thinking. When he, e.g., writes about 'potentialities, driven by the daimonic urge' (May, 1982, p. 240) we clearly see that his view is rooted in Freudian ideas.

This urge needs to be integrated into the personality, which in May's view is the purpose of psychotherapy – again undoubtedly an analytical position. As for Freud for May, too, the evil is an ontological, not only a moral problem. The Gnostic thesis of the failed creation returns (Safranski, 1999, p. 249).

May, in his efforts at reconciling Freud and the existentialists, turned his attention to motivation. His basic motivational construct is the daimonic as the entire system of motives, different for each individual which is thought to be composed of a collection of specific motives called daimons and has obvious parallels with Freud's id (see also Cooper, 2003, p. 84).

The term *daimonic,* from Greek δαιμονιον *[daimonion],* i.e., 'the divine, the divine power or little god' was earlier used by Xenophon, Socrates and Nietzsche (and influenced Schopenhauer's 'will to live' concept) to describe the warning inner voice of the deity, an ethical intuition (not to be mixed up with *demon,* which means an evil spirit).

Rollo May was convinced that the daimonic urge (not to be mixed with *demonic*) is a central motive for each individual to face life and the principal source of our potential to develop constructively as well as destructively. Unlike Rogers' actualising tendency, May's daimonic 'urge for self-affirmation is not in any a priori sense directionally set. It could be expressed either constructively or destructively' – that is (and here is no difference to Rogers) – 'humans are inherently capable of both good and evil' (Patterson, 2008, p. 29).

According to May it is important to integrate the daimonic forces; otherwise – if one daimon becomes so important that he takes over –

they result in destructive activities, with the 'daimonic possession' as a result. Therefore, May (1982) concludes that confronting these issues is crucial (p. 240). And he emphasises that 'the issue of not confronting evil is the most important error in the humanistic movement' (p. 249). Because – and here May (1969, p. 131) seems to be quite inconsistent – 'not to recognise the daimonic itself turns out to be daimonic, it makes us accomplices on the side of the destructive possession.' Why does May call destructive possession 'daimonic', if the daimonic is neither good nor evil in itself?

One sole source: The evil as the minor good

According to the other strand, the classical doctrine of both Greek and Christian philosophy the evil, the κακον, is not a principle of its own, it has no being. This is because e*sse qua esse bonum est*, all being as being is good (Augustine). Therefore the evil is a deficiency in being, it lacks full being: 'malum privatio essendi et boni' (Thomas Aquinas). The Latin word *malus* means 'small, minor, inferior'.

Strictly speaking, the imperfect *is* not. What *is*, as far as it *is*, is good and perfect. The evil is an absence of being that ought to *be* there, but *is* not. Thus it is στερησις *[steresis], privatio* (Latin *privare* means *deprive, rob of*). The evil is deprived of (full) being, it misses something, namely that what it should be. It is deprivation, imperfection, a defect of being, ultimately something that has no substance, no being, that does not exist. *To ουκ ον [To uk on]* (Origenes), *privatio entis* or *privatio essendi et boni*: The evil is the absence of what should be, of the being and the good. It is similar to darkness which is the absence of light and not something in its own right. Or like blindness: the organ is good, blindness is a lack of its functioning. Or a hole: a hole *is* not; it becomes the bigger the less there is. Aristotle's famous example is the deformed infant: they can only survive if they do not fall short of a minimum of being.

This is the thinking of many philosophers from Pythagoras, Plato, Epiktet, Augustine, Boethius, Dionysius Pseudo-Areopagita, Thomas Aquinas and Christian metaphysics to Leibnitz, Spinosa, Hegel, Goethe (see his famous drama *Faust*, 1808/1832, with Mephistopheles as the 'devil' who always aims at the evil and yet causes the good, vv 1336–1337), Heidegger, Buber and many, many others.

The Bible holds a similar conviction. After the creation 'God saw everything which he had made and it was very good' (Gen 1:31). The primeval narrative of the Fall of the Human Being (Gen 3) states that (a) the evil does not originate in God (b) nor is its origin in a counter-divine power – the devil is a fallen angel, a creature, and not another god (Schmid, 2000; 2001) – and (c) it is also not part of the created order: humanity is made in God's image (Schmid, 1998a). In the paradise there was no evil. The root cause of all evil is the human's voluntarily turning away from *the* good, i.e. God. This estrangement led to the inability to become perfect, to become, what we could be from ourselves. It's only God, and that means love, who can overcome the evil. Ultimately in a Judeo-Christian view, evil is the negation of the good.

And Martin Buber (1952, p. 192) writes: 'The evil cannot be done wholeheartedly; the good can only be done wholeheartedly'. The humans lie to, deceive to being when denying their true self. He coins the term '*Vergegnung*' instead of *Begegnung*, '*miscounter*' instead of *encounter*, the denial of encounter, going astray, missing each other instead of meeting.

Carl Rogers

The weltanschauung of Carl Rogers (1902–1987) is deeply rooted in this strand: Something could be there, but is not or not yet; the basically constructive nature of the formative and the actualising tendencies; the need of the Other for the actualizing tendency to work; the fundamentally constructive, trustworthy and forward moving human nature, as opposed to a beast to be tamed (by which he directly attacked Freud and Nietzsche) and the proactive direction of their movement under facilitative conditions; the voluntary choice; the fully functioning person who has all qualities of a person in fullness (as in the Bible's paradise lost) – and the really existing persons lacking some of these in different graduations, alienated, estranged from their true nature – from what could and should be, but is not; unconditional positive regard, the psychological technical term for love, as transcending negative assessment and self-assessment; etc.

Like May, one of the most important roots of Rogers' thinking, is in Christian belief. He had been brought up in a Christian tradition and had been a student of theology. 'I am influenced by the Judeo-Christian stream of thought', Rogers (1965, p. 10) confessed. Following Goldstein, he holds the idea that there is only one motivational force, the force of actualisation (see Rogers, 1951; 1963; Patterson, 2008, p. 31).

But, contrary to widespread misinterpretation, Rogers (1982, p. 254) does not postulate that humans are basically good. 'In my experience every person has the capacity for evil behaviour. I, and others, have had murderous and cruel impulses, desires to impose our will on others.'

Actualisation does not necessarily go in a prosocial direction. But Rogers saw it as an empirical observation that human beings have a potential to be constructive in an *individual and social* way and the actualising tendency makes people *naturally and spontaneously* grow in this direction (see Bohart, 2007), if – if the individual finds themselves in a facilitative relationship:

> If the elements making for growth are present, the actualizing tendency develops in positive ways. In the human these elements for growth are … a climate of psychological attitudes. (1982, pp. 253–4)

So whatever the evil might be, according to Rogers it is a matter not only of the individual or a matter of society only, but a matter of relationship.

Rogers was heavily criticised by many: 'Your viewpoint is devilishly innocent.' (Warren Bennis to Rogers, Film 1976). Despite such accusations that Rogers underrated the forces of evil (see Thorne, 2003, p. 79), Rogers was not naïve. It is ridiculous and against the facts to think Rogers did not recognise the 'dark side' or held too rosy a view of the human nature. But, different from others, he did find 'members of the human species as *essentially* constructive in their fundamental nature, but damaged by their experience'. (Rogers, 1981, p. 238)

> It disturbs me to be thought of as an optimist. My whole professional experience has been with the dark and often sordid side of life, and I know, better than most, the incredibly destructive behavior of which man is capable. Yet that same professional

experience has forced upon me the realization that man, when you know him deeply, in his worst and most troubled states, is not evil or demonic. (1958, p. 17)

The presence of terrorism, hostility, and aggression are urgent in our days. I am very well aware of the incredible amount of destructive, cruel, malevolent behavior in our todays's world – from the threats of war to the senseless violence in the streets. It is cultural influences which are the major factor in our evil behaviors. (1981, p. 238)

I am quite aware that out of defensiveness and inner fear individuals can and do behave in ways which are incredibly cruel, horribly destructive, immature, regressive, anti-social, hurtful. Yet one of the most refreshing and invigorating parts of my experience is to work with such individuals and to discover the strongly positive directional tendencies which exist in them, as in all of us, at the deepest levels. (1961, p. 27)

Rogers summarised his conviction:

I do not discover man to be well characterised, in his basic nature, by such terms as *fundamentally hostile, antisocial, destructive, evil.*

I do not discover man to be, in his basic nature, completely without a nature, a tabula rasa on which *anything* may be written, nor malleable putty which can be shaped in *any* form.

I do not discover man to be essentially a perfect being, sadly warped and corrupted by society.

In my experience I have discovered man to have characteristics which seem inherent in his species, and the terms which have at different times seemed to me descriptive of these characteristics are such terms as *positive, forward-moving, constructive, realistic, trustworthy.* (1957, p. 403)

He expressed his conviction quite similarly in exchanges with Paul Tillich, May's teacher in Union Theological Seminary in New York.

People sometimes say to me, 'What if you create a climate of freedom? A man might use that freedom to become completely evil or antisocial.' I don't find that to be true, and that is one of the

things that makes me feel that … in a relationship of real freedom
the individual tends to move not only toward deeper self-
understanding, but toward more social behavior. (Rogers and
Tillich, 1966, p. 68)

And in his review of a book by the theologian Reinhold Niebuhr
he wrote:

It is in his [Niebuhr's] conception of the basic deficiency of the
individual self that I find my experience utterly at variance. He is
quite clear that the 'original sin' is self love […] I could not differ
more deeply from the notion that self love is the fundamental and
pervasive 'sin'. (Rogers, 1956, p. 14)

About the Freudian Karl Menninger Rogers said:

When a Freudian such as Karl Menninger tells me (as he has, in a
discussion of this issue) that he perceives man as … 'innately
destructive', I can only shake my head in wonderment. (Rogers,
1957, p. 405)

To sum it up, here is his creed in the formulation (from his 1957
'note on the nature of man'):

- The human being is not fundamentally evil,
- not without a nature,
- not essentially perfect.
- Constructiveness is inherent in the human species.

In a word: 'I find in my experience no such *innate* tendency toward
evil.' (Rogers, 1982, p. 253, italics mine)

Evil – the price of freedom
But, if the human being's nature is essentially constructive, this,
however, again raises the question: *Unde malum?* Whence the
evil?

Rogers' answer to the *unde malum problem* does not only reflect
the traditional Western position; his view 'is the essence of a
phenomenological position, when carried to its logical conclusion',
as Brian Thorne (2003, p. 86) remarks.

Rogers states that whether evil impulses and desires become behaviour depends on (a) *social conditioning* and/or (b) *voluntary choice*. With this statement Rogers acknowledges both the power of imposed conditions of worth, of forces outside our awareness *and* the free will. With stressing the human being's capacity of free choice he rejects both the absolute behaviourist position and the analytic position of the overall rule of the unconscious (see Thorne, 2003, pp. 86–7), although like the psychodynamic theoreticians Rogers acknowledged the social conditioning in early childhood – see his remarks on Hitler (1982, p. 254) and Alice Miller's investigations of Hitler's upbringing, as quoted by Tony Merry (1995, pp. 31–3) in his chapter 'If people are so constructive. Why do they do so destructive things' (pp. 29–34).

It is worth noticing that May, in his rebuttal (1982), does only refer to one of the elements, namely the culture, and blames Rogers that he does not see the individual's responsibility – thus clearly ignoring Rogers' stance about the free will.

The traditional answer to the question why we do have the problem of the moral evil is the freedom of the human being. If the human is free, they have the freedom of choice, the free will. Its misuse is, according to Kant, the evil. Rogers is definitely in the tradition of those who see the evil as the 'price of freedom' (Safranski, 1999) as part of the 'drama of freedom'.

Consequences for psychotherapeutic practice

Rogers rightly writes that the question of 'origin makes a great deal of difference philosophically' (Rogers, 1982, p. 253), but of course there are consequences of the different images of the human being for the practice of psychotherapy, too. What are they?

May's answer is that 'aspects of evil need to be brought out in therapy.' (May, 1982, p.17) So, it is only consequent that 'the daimonic needs to be directed and channelled' (1969, p. 126) and integrated (1969/1982).

To take care 'to integrate something' means to have a goal for the client. Not unlike Fritz Perls, the co-founder of Gestalt therapy, with his background in Freudian analysis, Rollo May could not think of a therapy where the therapist does not have to guide the client in some way and to confront them with matters the therapist thinks are crucial for the client. Despite their move towards existential, humanistic, phenomenological convictions neither Perls nor May made the radical shift to a fully *client*-centred psychotherapy. (Yet, even so the question remains, why it is considered necessary in therapy to stress the confrontation with evil and not the confrontation with good.)

Rogers' answer to the issue of therapy is that of course the evil is a subject in therapy as every other subject.

The avoidance of aggressive, hostile, negative, destructive, evil issues, as critically annotated e.g., by reviewers at the 'Wisconsin Project' (Rogers et al., 1967), but not at all only there, is clearly a malpractice, a professional error on the part of the therapist – quite often probably because of the missing confrontation with the own 'dark side'. But it is definitely not at all something that is inherent to the image of the human being in the PCA.

It goes without saying that some person-centred people tend to avoid confrontation, aggression and dealing with so-called negative feelings or thoughts and I've repeatedly learned that in these cases it is the seemingly harmless image of the approach that attracted them – a result of watering down of what appeared to be too radical a challenge. It seems also obvious that Rogers and others needed time to dare to take the risk to encounter these sides of their clients in the required depth. As *en-counter*, a term that originally was used for hostile meetings only – note that there is *counter* in the word! – psychotherapy is always the risk to be surprised by the Other and to meet the challenge of the unexpected (see Schmid, 1996; Schmid and Mearns, 2006).

Two divergent positions ?

Both men have a lot of similarities: among others a move from theology to psychology (in a way Rogers is the Catholic and May the Protestant in this debate), both influenced by Otto Rank and his theory of will, both dedicated to the idea of a genuinely humanistic, existence-based psychology, both concerned with political implications.

While May believed that humans have both constructive and destructive *inherent* impulses, Rogers was convinced of the constructive and pro-social nature of the inherent actualising tendency and stressed that what is generally thought of and referred to as evil is, more accurately, an outward expression of a person's internal estrangement between the actualising tendency and their striving to self-actualisation.

Thus there are clearly two quite different anthropological positions originating in different philosophical backgrounds with different practical consequences. But they are more alike than they appear at first sight, because both are grounded in conventional ontological thinking.

Being-centred or person-centred?

Mearns' objection

A comment by Dave Mearns on the issue sheds light on the fact that contemporary men and women no longer find traditional ontological categories to provide sufficient solutions to their experiences. His answer to the *unde malum* problem is anxiety.

Mearns' – as he says 'disparaging' – definition of evil comprehends it as 'a hypothetical construct used to describe someone whom we fear and whom we do not understand' (Mearns and Thorne, 2000, p. 59).

This – admittedly rude – position indicates among other things that a discussion of the question whence the evil derives – a question that comes from experience, not from a philosophy that lost touch with the real world – that a discussion of this question in abstract ontological categories might well be outdated, because we no longer are thinking about our experiencing and our existing in those conceptions. On the contrary we need existential answers to existential questions.

Ontological or dialogic ?

Both May and Rogers discussed the problem still in traditional ontological categories. Both did hold that there is a human nature (Bohart, 2009) and discussed the issue around the issue of the human nature in a one-sided, substantialistic way. Both of them were occupied with the question: what is *in* the individual?

Consequently thought through in the light of a personalistic or dialogic anthropology as it is appropriate for a *person*-centred approach and a *dialogical* understanding of psychotherapy (Schmid, 2006) Rogers' and May's being rooted in traditional ontological categories or even being captives of such thinking with the idea of an existing or non-existing evil *in* the individual, with the idea of an evil substance that exists or does not exist, is inappropriate for a truly personal understanding of the human being, a comprehension of the human as a person, as it is the underlying idea of the *person*-centred approach.

This is not only true for May's thinking, which is close to Kant in its belief that the evil is inherent to the human being. Here also Rogers was inconsistent. Not only May (as Schneider, 2009, thinks), in this respect *both* took a 'being-centred' view. Although Rogers responded to May's repeatedly uttered demand for ontology: 'Rollo, if you want an ontology you write one. I don't feel the need for it' (Kirschenbaum, 2007, p. 236), he obviously thought in ontological categories.

Paradoxically, when he refuses the idea that the human being has 'to fulfil an evil nature' (Rogers, 1982, p. 253), he seems to be more concerned with ontology than May.

Although he took a non-traditional stance in his epistemology where he came to question 'a' reality, a 'real' nature of reality (Rogers, 1978), thus proving to be one of the first constructivists, he did not do the respective step in the area of anthropology that we discuss here.

Now, almost 30 years after the debate, we do not need to repeat their admittedly thought-provoking stances but we need to proceed and advance our philosophy.

A personal-dialogic position

Personal anthropology

Definitely, the development of the philosophy of the human being, the anthropology, went from *being-centred* to *person-centred*, i.e. from metaphysics to existentialism, phenomenology, personalism and dialogical philosophy and not the other way round. The question at stake for today's consciousness – after the paradigm shift from general philosophy to a humanistic anthropology – is not about *being as such* but about *personal being (Personales Sein,*

Wucherer-Huldenfeld, 1994/1997). This is a still ongoing process and a perspective to be continuously developed.

The adequate question for anthropology and therefore for a genuine humane psychology – equalling the paradigmatic shift from natural science to human science – is no longer w*hat is the human being?* a question with which Kant introduced philosophical anthropology as fundamental philosophy, but it is *who is this (specific) human being?* and, in the light of dialogical philosophy, *who are* you*?* as the question of relationship from person to person and thus of encounter, interrelatedness and dialogue (see Schmid, 1991, pp. 19–21; 1994; 1996; 1998a; b; c; 2006; 2007a). The *quid* (what?) addresses the essence, the nature, the *quis* (who?) addresses the person both in their substantiality and interrelatedness.

So the question is not *was Rogers being-centred enough?* (Schneider, 2009), but it has to be: *was Rogers person-centred enough?*

In order to think genuinely *person*-centred we need to understand the notion of the term *person*. The issue at stake is about being and becoming a person, personalisation.

The meaning of 'person'

Philosophically the person-centred approach is founded out of the conviction that the image of the human being most adequate to our experience we have been developing so far in the history of humankind is to regard him and her as a person. To be a person means that the human being is intrinsically and dialectically both substantial and relational: being from oneself and thus autonomous, and being from relationship and thus interdependent. Human beings have an innate capacity, need and tendency to develop on their own and in relationships. Both autonomy and interrelatedness constitute the one human nature. Thus the two essential dimensions of person-centred anthropology are independence and interconnectedness. This image of the human being is the essential conclusion of the process of reflection about ourselves in the European tradition during more than two millennia from the Jews and Greeks via the Muslims until today. Therefore to be a person depicts an understanding of the human as a substantial-relational being, autonomous *and* interdependent, characterised by self-responsibility *and* solidarity.

In the development of the PCA genuinely unfolding Rogers' personality theory and theory of interpersonal relationships, an improved realisation of the relational dimension of personhood within the paradigm has been achieved, whether you term it encounter approach, meeting at relational depth, relationship-oriented approach or dialogical. Such an image of the human being with its profoundness and radicalism and the dialectical balance of substantiality and relationality can only be found in a genuine *person*-centred approach and is the foundation of the identity of this approach to therapy and the state of the art of PCT in theory and practice today.

And such a consequently personal anthropology overcomes thinking in conventional ontological categories.

The person and evil

From a phenomenological point of view this of course includes the issue of what we call 'evil' and the 'dark or negative side' of human experience, imagination and behaviour. The understanding of the human as person implies the challenge of an authentic confrontation with and the necessity of taking a stance towards these phenomenological facts. If we experience those phenomena – by our fellow humans' behaviour, by our own ideas, wishes and actions – then it is a matter of authenticity to deal with them – philosophically, theoretically and in the therapeutic practice. This means to take seriously that the evil is foremost an elementary *experience* to a human being and not so much a matter of terminology or metaphysical discussion.

Thus, from a personal perspective, *evil is to avoid personalization,* to not actualise the potential of fully being and becoming a person regarding the substantial as well as the relational dimension of personhood, which means to avoid authenticity and to avoid solidarity, to avoid becoming who you are and to avoid encountering other human beings, to avoid autonomy and responsibility, to avoid sovereignty and engagement, to ignore one's possibilities and to ignore dialogue and the fundamental human We – in a word: evil is to escape from genuinely being and becoming a person.

In considering both dimensions of personhood and therefore fully acknowledging the fact that as human beings we are not only *in* relationships but we *are* relationship (Schmid, 2006), only such a perspective overcomes what Levinas (1957, p. 189) called 'egology', i.e. being concerned with the I (e.g., 'What do I have to do as a therapist?'). Only a truly *client*-centred perspective grasps towards a self-understanding of being-for. The relevance for a genuinely client- or person-centred therapy is obvious.

Ratio mali, the reason of evil, is not to be found in objective substantial realities, but in personal and interpersonal qualities and attitudes (see Rotter, 1993; pp. 104–5). It is a *no* to all perspectives of personalization – towards oneself and towards the others, a refusal to both authentic self-realisation and self-fulfilment and authentic relationship as being-for-each-other by being-with and being-counter each other (Schmid and Mearns, 2006; Mearns and Schmid, 2006). It is the inauthentic responding or the denial of responding to the dialogical situation we find ourselves in in this world. It is particularly the unwillingness to deal with the unknown, the strange (Schmid, in print).

Evil as deprivation of love
Evil is everything that opposes personal being. If the meaning of being consists in being-for-each-other, we don't talk about anything else but love. Evil is opposition to love.

Therefore, in other words – and with all cautiousness and carefulness because of the multiple meanings of the word 'love' – evil is the failure to love oneself as well as the other. Note: to love in the meaning of αγαπη *[agape]*as Rogers (1951; 1962) used the term, a personal posture that he carefully and in detail described. In a personal-dialogical perspective love is the fulfilment of dialogue (Rombold, 1984, II, p. 86).

> To love means to open ourselves to the negative as well as the positive – to grief, sorrow, and disappointment as well as to joy, fulfilment, and an intensity of consciousness we did not know was possible before.' (May, 1969, p. 100)

Unde malum? From a philosophy of the person's stance the answer is *privatio amoris,* deprivation of love. It is evil to deprive oneself and others of respect, regard, acknowledgment as a person, in a word to withhold love towards oneself and others.

The result is definitely not an overly positive view of human nature. We all owe each other and ourselves love. To not acknowledge this interpersonal condition in the therapeutic encounter and dialogue is, theologically speaking a sin, from the point of view of psychotherapy science it is professional blunder. The place of the so-called 'negative' in the therapeutic process based on an existential view of an encounter-oriented psychotherapy that truly deserves the name 'person-centred' lies in the *conditionality of positive regard*, in the deprivation of love (an idea that can be found in both Freud and Rogers – see above).

This is not only true for the cocooned client-therapist relationship (which would mean that the problem of evil is reduced to an individual phenomenon). This is also true for groups and for society as a whole (and only then the structurally evil can be reflected). And so it turns out that the question of evil is also and today predominantly a question for social psychology, sociology and politics, because 'psychotherapy is political or it is not psychotherapy'. (Schmid, 2007b)

References

Bohart, AC (2007) The actualizing person. In: M Cooper, M O'Hara, PF Schmid, G Wyatt, (eds) *The Handbook of Person-centred Psychotherapy and Counselling* (pp. 47–63). Houndmills: Palgrave.

Bohart, AC (2009) Abstract to the APA symposium 'Luminaries and Legacies: Carl Rogers and Rollo May', Toronto.

Buber, M (1952) *Bilder von Gut und Böse*, (4th edn 1986; orig. 1952). Heidelberg: Lambert Schneider.

Cooper, M (2003) *Existential Therapies.* London: Sage.

Freud, S (1920) Jenseits des Lustprinzips. In: *Gesammelte Werke, 13,* 1–69. Frankfurt/M.: Fischer (1999; orig. 1920).

Goethe, JW von (1808/1832). *Faust. Der Tragödie erster und zweiter Teil.* Stuttgart: Reclam (1966; orig.: part I 1808; part II 1832).

Kirschenbaum, H (2007) *Carl Rogers: Life and work.* Ross-on-Wye: PCCS Books.

Kirschenbaum, H & Land Henderson, V (1989) *Carl Rogers: Dialogues.* Boston: Houghton Mifflin.

Levinas, E (1957) Die Philosophie und die Idee des Unendlichen. In: *Die Spur des Anderen: Untersuchung zur Phänomenologie und Sozial-philosophie* (pp. 185–208). Freiburg: Alber (1983; orig. 1957).

May, R (1969) *Love and Will.* New York: Dell.

May, R (1982) The problem of evil: An open letter to Carl Rogers. In: H Kirschenbaum & V Land Henderson (eds) *Carl Rogers: Dialogues.* Boston: Houghton Mifflin (1989, pp. 239–51; orig.: *Journal of Humanistic Psychology, 22,* 10–21).

Mearns, D & Thorne, B (2000) *Person-centred Therapy Today: New frontiers in theory and practice.* London: Sage.

Mearns, D & Schmid, PF (2006) Being-with and being-counter: Relational depth – The challenge of fully meeting the client. *Person-Centered and Experiential Psychotherapies, 5,* 255–65.

Merry, T (1995) *Invitation to Person-centred Psychology.* London: Whurr.

Patterson, CH (2008) *Understanding Psychotherapy: Fifty years of client-centred theory and practice.* Ross-on-Wye: PCCS Books.

Rogers, CR (1951) *Client-centered Therapy: Its current practice, implications, and theory.* Boston: Houghton Mifflin.

Rogers, CR (1956) Review of Reinhold Niebuhr's 'The self and the dramas of history'. *Chicago Theological Seminary Register XLVI,* 1, 13–14.

Rogers, CR (1957) A note on the 'nature of man'. In: H Kirschenbaum & V Land Henderson (eds) *The Carl Rogers Reader.* Boston: Houghton Mifflin (1989, 219–35; orig.: *Journal of Counseling Psychology, 4,* 199–203.

Rogers, CR (1958) Concluding comment [In: R Niebuhr & CR Rogers. A discussion (of R Niebuhr's 'The self and the dramas of history') by BM Loomer, WM Horton & H Hofmann]. *Pastoral Psychology, 9*(85), 15–17.

Rogers, CR (1961) The process equation of psychotherapy. *American Journal of Psychotherapy, 15,* 27–45

Rogers, CR (1962) The interpersonal relationship: The core of guidance. In: CR Rogers & B Stevens, *Person to Person: The problem of being human* (pp. 89–104). Moab: Real People.

Rogers, CR (1963) The actualizing tendency in relation to 'motives' and to consciousness. In: MR Jones (ed) *Nebraska Symposion on Motivation* (pp. 1–24). Lincoln, NE: University of Nebraska Press.

Rogers, CR (1965) A humanistic conception of man. In: R Farson (ed) *Science and Human Affairs* (pp. 18–31). Palo Alto, CA: Science and Behavior Books.

Rogers, CR (Film 1976) *Reflections: With Carl Rogers and Warren Bennis.* APGA. Psychological Films.

Rogers, CR (1978) Do we need 'a' reality? *Dawnpoint, 1*(2), 6–9.

Rogers, CR (1981) Notes on Rollo May. In: H Kirschenbaum & V Land Henderson (eds) *Carl Rogers: Dialogues.* Boston: Houghton Mifflin

(1989, 237–9; orig.: *Perspectives*, *2*(1), 1.

Rogers, CR (1982) Reply to Rollo May's Letter to Carl Rogers. In: H Kirschenbaum & V Land Henderson (eds) *Carl Rogers: Dialogues.* Boston: Houghton Mifflin (1989, 251–5; orig.: *Journal of Humanistic Psychology*, *22*(4), 85–9.

Rogers, CR, Gendlin, ET, Kiesler, DJ & Truax, CB (1967) *The Therapeutic Relationship and its Impact: A study of psychotherapy with schizophrenics.* Madison, WI: University of Wisconsin Press.

Rogers CR & Tillich, P (1966) Paul Tillich and Carl Rogers – a dialogue. In: H Kirschenbaum & V Land Henderson (eds) *Carl Rogers:Dialogues* (pp. 64–78). Boston: Houghton Mifflin (1989; orig.: San Diego:San Diego State College).

Rombold, G (1984) Anthropologie I+II. Unpublished manuscript.

Rotter, H (1993) *Person und Ethik: Zur Grundlegung der Moraltheologie.* Innsbruck: Tyrolia.

Safranski, R (1999) *Das Böse oder Das Drama der Freiheit.* Frankfurt/M.: Fischer (orig. 1997).

Schmid, PF (1991) Souveränität und Engagement: Zu einem personzentrierten Verständis von 'Person'. In: CR Rogers and PF Schmid, *Person-zentriert: Grundlagen von Theorie und Praxis* (pp. 15–164). Main: Grünewald.

Schmid, PF (1994) *Personzentrierte Gruppenpsychotherapie: Ein Handbuch. Vol. I: Solidarität und Autonomie.* Cologne: EHP.

Schmid, PF (1996) *Personzentrierte Gruppenpsychotherapie in der Praxis: Ein Handbuch. Vol. II: Die Kunst der Begegnung.* Paderborn: Junfermann.

Schmid, PF (1998a) *Im Anfang ist Gemeinschaft. Vol. III: Personzentrierte Gruppenarbeit in Seelsorge und Praktischer Theologie. Vol. III.* Stuttgart: Kohlhammer.

Schmid, PF (1998b) 'On becoming a Person-centered therapy': A person-centred understanding of the person. In: B Thorne & E Lambers (eds) *Person-Centred Therapy: A European perspective* (pp. 38–52). London: Sage.

Schmid, PF (1998c) 'Face to face': The art of encounter. In: B Thorne & E Lambers (eds) *Person-centred Therapy: A European perspective* (pp. 74–90). London: Sage.

Schmid, PF (2000) Personalisation oder Mephisto wird Supervisor. Play. Symposion,Wie führe ich ein ehrenwertes Leben [How to lead an honourable life], Vienna, 2000. *http://www.pfs-online.at/papers/ 50theater.htm* [retrieved February 21, 2010].

Schmid, PF (2001) 'Puzzling you is the nature of my game'. Von der

Faszination und dem Verdrängen des Bösen. *Diakonia, 32*(2), 77–83.

Schmid, PF (2006) *'In the beginning there is community': Implications* and *challenges of the belief in a triune God and a person-centred approach.* Norwich: Norwich Centre Occasional Publication Series.

Schmid, PF (2007a) The anthropological and ethical foundations of person-centred therapy. In: M Cooper et al. (eds) *The Handbook of Person-centred Psychotherapy and Counselling* (pp. 30–46). Houndsmill: Palgrave Macmillan.

Schmid, PF (2007b) Psychotherapy is political or it is not psychotherapy: The actualizing tendency as personalizing tendency. Keynote lecture, 3rd BAPCA Conference: 'Person Centred Approach: Past, Present and Future', Cirencester, UK.

Schmid, PF (in print) Beyond question and answer: The challenge to facilitate freedom. Proceedings of the International Conference PC Counseling & Psychotherapy Today: Evolution & Challenges, 2009, Athens.

Schmid, PF & Mearns, D (2006) Being-with and being-counter: Person-centered psychotherapy as an in-depth co-creative process of personalization. *Person-Centered and Experiential Psychotherapies, 5,* 174–90.

Schneider, K (2009) Ontology and depth: Rollo May's inseparable duo. Abstract to the APA symposium 'Luminaries and Legacies: Carl Rogers and Rollo May', Toronto, 2009.

Thorne, B (2003) *Carl Rogers* (2nd edn). London: Sage.

Wucherer-Huldenfeld, AK (1994/1997) *Ursprüngliche Erfahrung und personales Sein.* (Vol I: 1994 / Vol. II: 1997) Wien: Böhlau.

Wucherer-Huldenfeld, AK (2009) Wie sollen wir mit dem Übel umgehen? Skizze einer praktischen 'Theodizee'. Unpublished manuscript.

Contributors

Jan Hawkins is a person-centred therapist, supervisor and trainer working in private practice in London. She has published a number of articles and chapters in other books on aspects of person-centred practice as well as a her own book *Voices of the Voiceless* (PCCS Books, 2002), the aim of which is to encourage person-centred therapists to engage with people who have learning disabilities. When not working Jan is often to be found leading a choir; finding the sharing of music and song wonderfully therapeutic.

Mia Leijssen is psychotherapist and Professor at the Psychology Department of the University of Leuven. She teaches client-centered psychotherapy, counselling skills, and professional ethics at Masters level, and psychotherapy training in the Postgraduate Program. She has practised client-centred/experiential/existential psychotherapy since 1973. She is a mother and grandmother.

Jeff Leonardi: After counselling training at Aston in Birmingham (1978–1979), I worked as a counsellor, supervisor and trainer for ten years, during which time I also pursued, or was pursued by, training for ordination as a priest in the Church of England. I served as a parish priest in Cumbria from 1988–1997 and was then appointed to my present post as Bishop's Adviser for Pastoral Care and Counselling and Associate Minister in a cluster of rural parishes in the Lichfield Diocese in Staffordshire. In 2009 I was awarded a doctorate, 'Partners or Adversaries: Christianity and the Person-centred Approach' by the University of East Anglia.

Dave Mearns is Emeritus Professor at the University of Strathclyde. In 2010 the University Counselling Unit, which he founded, was given the Charlotte and Karl Buhler Award of the American

Psychological Association for its contribution to Humanistic Psychology. Professor Mearns has authored seven books, including *Person-Centred Counselling in Action* (Sage, 2007) and *Person-Centred Therapy Today* (Sage, 2000) with Brian Thorne. Dave and Brian have known and worked with each other for 34 years. They have frequently been described as 'the odd couple' and by one student as 'the bishop and the poacher', attributions that point to their obvious differences but miss their shared passion and commitment.

Judy Moore is Director of the University Counselling Service and Director of the Centre for Counselling Studies at the University of East Anglia. She trained as a counsellor in the mid-1980s and has worked in student counselling since then. Throughout much of the 1990s she was a core tutor on the UEA postgraduate diploma in counselling and has subsequently taught on the Centre's diploma in focusing and experiential psychotherapy as well as supervising counselling research students. She is particularly interested in the development of person-centred theory and how cultural and contextual factors impact upon counselling process. She has co-edited (with Campbell Purton) *Spirituality and Counselling: Experiential and theoretical perspectives* (PCCS Books, 2006) and (with Ruth Roberts) *Counselling in Organisational Settings* (Learning Matters, 2010).

Campbell Purton works at the Centre for Counselling Studies at the University of East Anglia, where he has designed and taught several courses in focusing-oriented psychotherapy. He is at present involved in establishing focusing-oriented therapy in China and in exploring resonances between focusing and Buddhist meditation. He is the author of *Person-Centred Therapy: The Focusing-Oriented Approach* (Palgrave Macmillan, 2004) and of *The Focusing-Oriented Counselling Primer* (PCCS Books, 2007). He has co-edited (with Judy Moore) *Spirituality and Counselling: Experiential and theoretical perspectives* (PCCS Books, 2006).

Peter F. Schmid, Univ. Doz., HSProf., Mag. Dr., University of Graz, Austria; director of the person-centred department at the Sigmund Freud University, Vienna; Faculty Member Saybrook

Graduate School and Research Center, San Francisco, USA; co-director Academy for Counselling and Psychotherapy of the Institute for Person-Centred Studies (IPS of APG), Vienna; person-centred psychotherapist in private practice. Recipient of the Carl Rogers Award of the American Psychological Association (APA) 2009. For further information consult: www.pfs-online.at.

Alison Shoemark: I trained as a person-centred therapist in the late 1980s. Along with the profound experience of training, my background in palliative care nursing and working with people living 'at the edge' for some other reason, has, more than anything, taught me to have a deep appreciation of life and of the value of striving for honest and genuine relationships. Mindfulness has been a key element of my development as a person and with its focus on acceptance is central also to my counselling practice.